SELF-DEFENSE:

The Womanly Art of Self-Care, Intuition and Choice

by DEBBIE LEUNG

photographs by MARY FITZGERALD

R&M PRESS · TACOMA · WASHINGTON

SELF-DEFENSE:
The Womanly Art of Self-Care, Intuition and Choice

by DEBBIE LEUNG

First edition.

ISBN 0-929838-08-4

LC 91-061404

Published by R&M Press, Tacoma, Washington 98402

Printed in the United States of America

Printed with soybean ink on recycled paper

DEDICATION

*To women everywhere, always rising to face adversity
with courage and perseverance.*

TABLE OF CONTENTS

ACKNOWLEDGMENTS

It took the hard work, support, and encouragement of many people to make this book a reality.

Its production was funded by the Office of Crime Victim Advocacy in Washington state's Department of Community Development. Much is owed to FIST's community supporters, especially Tyra Lindquist (Safeplace), Debbie Ruggles (Central WA Comprehensive Mental Health), Sheri Gray (WA Coalition of Sexual Assault Programs), Pam Norris (YWCA), and Nancy Koppleman and Gail Martin (The Evergreen State College) who took time out of their busy schedules to write letters in support of this project.

Mer Calderone was a valuable partner throughout the book writing process. She is a FIST member who researched the facts, provided ideas for all aspects of the book's production, scrutinized the manuscript, did her time on data entry, and still thought to ask, "How are YOU doing?" She always maintained her quiet friendly manner and sense of humor when I'd bother her at all hours about references for more gory details. I owe a lot to Mer.

Other FIST members, Staci Cotler, Cathy Burnstead, Lea Mitchell, Debbie Nickerson, and Lisa Kidd, also took time out of their busy lives to review draft manuscripts. Eunice Torres Santiago, Karen Huntsberger, Sara Rideout, and Anne Ellsworth are community members who made valuable comments from their own perspectives and encouraged me to keep going.

The models in the photos were great sports. Charlene Hegsted, Eunice Torres Santiago, Gretchen Steiger, Clarissa Starks-Coates, Bill Spearance, and Walter Bryant volunteered many awkward hours in order to create the scenes photographed so well by Mary Fitzgerald. Thanks also go to Gretchen, John, and the folks of Cascadia Research Collective for providing the locations for the "assaults".

Many of these people and others, too, were there for me when I needed resources, had questions, or wanted an opinion. Thank you for your time and enthusiasm.

I cannot forget to thank my mate who tolerated my moodiness while I holed up for months in front of the computer. Chores were left undone and nobody got much attention while I worked frantically to meet deadlines. A big hug of appreciation is in order.

Finally, this book is a reality because of the FIST collective's belief in this project, confidence that I could pull it off, and commitment to assault prevention education. The ideas in this book evolved from a process I participated in with many others. This process is ongoing and the ideas continually evolve as FIST members make observations, contemplate, and discuss the issues and their experiences. The ideas are greatly influenced by the women who attend our classes and others also working to build a world free of violence.

INTRODUCTION

My first exposure to "self-defense" was in a women's karate class in 1978. Not knowing what to expect, I tagged along with several co-workers. I went partly out of curiosity and partly for adventure. But when I look back, I realize that something deep in my being must have also drawn me to that first class because, after 13 years, I continue to participate in the martial arts and the movement to end assaults against women.

My commitment to women's self-defense and martial arts practice, now centered on kung-fu, led me down separate paths. The cultural context of my martial art is important to me and its practice continues to enrich my life in many ways. One benefit is that it has made me a better self-defense teacher. However, the foundation and content of FIST's self-defense programs for women are not about martial art.

In 1979, several members of my first karate class started FIST (Feminists In Self-Defense Training) in Olympia, Washington because we wanted greater freedom to develop programs accessible to larger numbers of women. Karate training was costly, time consuming, and unrealistic for many mothers. Its emphasis on physical skills did not apply to the full scope of violence women faced. Many women did not feel that it met their needs for prevention and avoidance.

FIST was founded on the belief that women of all ages, sizes, physical abilities, and cultural and economic backgrounds, have the right and ability to defend themselves successfully. Its programs differ from most self-defense programs by being based on women's experiences with violence, learning self-defense, and resisting assault successfully. They empower women to trust their instincts and use their abilities.

As a small, collectively organized volunteer agency, FIST has taught many women about assault prevention. We consistently find that most women, including ourselves, have encountered some form of violence in our lives and most have stories to tell about successful escapes. Women have shared a wide range of strategies that worked for them. The testimonials and generalizations about women in this book come from my experience and that of other FIST teachers working with women on assault prevention. I wish all women could be in my place to hear all the stories women tell because I am sure that then, women would share my conviction that we are all capable of defending ourselves with success.

This book is based on FIST's philosophy of self-defense for women. Because women are usually assaulted by men, the male gender is used when referring to assailants in this book. Research findings on this subject are presented in Chapter 3. Most people think of "self-defense" as escaping assault by fighting off attackers with punches and kicks. These skills are most easily described with photos. Looking only at the photos in this book, however, will give the reader a narrow glimpse of the full range of self-defense options covered. In addition to escape tactics, options also include prevention, avoidance, deterrence, and survival skills.

FIST views the primary aspect of prevention as having accurate information about assault. This information, in contrast to the myths about assault that pervade our society, allows us to realistically plan for our safety. Avoidance means taking action to keep assaults from being initiated when our senses, both physical and intuitive, identify an assailant contemplating assault. Once an assailant begins the process of asserting dominance, communicating confidence and assertiveness can keep the assault from escalating and is a primary factor in deterrence. Too often, we forget that the most critical aspect of facing violence is surviving it. Tools for survival help us maintain a sense of dignity and self-worth during an assault and can help us recover faster afterwards.

This book is written to speak to women, from one to another, by addressing the kinds of violence we face and the feelings and experiences we have as we learn to defend our safety. Many readers have already endured abuse and assault. It is common to flash back or feel strong emotions when thinking about assault as we do while learning about self-defense. I encourage you to take care of yourselves by talking to people, keeping a journal of thoughts, doing something fun, gardening, bicycling, or whatever you need to do to work through those emotions. The Appendix has ideas for resources that may be helpful.

My purpose in writing this book is to expose the truth about the violence women face and to build on the wealth of experiences women have had with successful resistance. It is time we drown out the messages we are told about not being able to defend ourselves and stand up proudly for what we have done, celebrate our successes, and share them with each other. Let's use this information to create our own destinies, ones that are free from violence.

FOREWORD

As I write this book, interest in self-defense is high among women in my community. Reports circulate about a mysterious attacker assaulting women walking alone at night. These assaults occurred in a quiet respectable neighborhood where several of my friends live, work, and play. Women want to learn self-defense because of the fear these assaults instill. The fear feels immobilizing and they want to stop feeling helpless. Some are angry that this man is restraining them from participating in their normal activities. They want to safely walk the streets at night.

Faceless men lurking in shadows are not the only reason women seek self-defense information. Women who have been assaulted, usually by someone they knew, want to prevent an assault from occurring again. Past experience with assault can motivate women to learn self-defense skills to feel more control over their lives and be more empowered.

Women also look to self-defense for practical options when feeling intimidated, harassed, manipulated, abused, insecure, or vulnerable. For some women, the main obstacle to protecting their safety is being able to express their needs. Protecting children and feeling safer in a new job or new community are other reasons women seek self-defense skills.

Fear, assault, and abuse (emotional and/or physical) are constant realities for most women. We look over our shoulders, wonder what *that man* is thinking, and worry about the possibility of assault in our everyday activities. Many women turn to self-defense for a change.

1
IS SELF-DEFENSE FOR ME?

Many who teach or talk about self-defense are asked, "Are you going to show us some karate?" This link with martial arts makes learning self-defense a dubious option for many women. Fears about hurting and injuring others, even attackers, and being unable to physically keep up are common. Participating in strenuous physical activity after a lifetime of not being athletic can be intimidating, especially for women who were taught that it is unladylike. The time and economic commitment for learning a martial art are large. In addition, the issue of self-defense relates so closely to abuse and assault that thinking, talking, and doing something about it can feel especially frightening and risky in a male-dominated activity such as martial arts.

Some women took a big step and learned self-defense in martial arts schools. Although our lives are greatly enriched by practicing a martial art, we feel a need to share our skills in a more practical manner that can reach larger numbers of women. After years of training, talking to each other, and working in agencies supporting victims of sexual assault and domestic violence, some of us began to think about "self-defense" in a new way.

A Women's Definition of Self-Defense

Our new concept of self-defense was influenced most by the women in our communities who confronted and survived violence. Their stories are corroborated by current research on assault against women. Women's experiences with abuse and assault together with our experiences learning to defend ourselves are reflected in a new definition of self-defense, a women's definition.

Self-defense is a way of nurturing ourselves by caring about our own safety and the safety of others. It involves intuition and making choices. We can use it to create a safe, supportive, and caring environment. Self-defense skills and strategies are much more than methods for defending against attackers. They help improve the overall quality of everyday life for women.

The skills that make up this approach to self-defense have many uses. Most important, they enhance our ability, as women, to cultivate our awareness of ourselves, relationships with others, and enjoyment of the world when used on a regular basis in situations that are not potentially threatening. They help us have more control over our lives. All women, including those with limited physical ability, can improve their lives with these skills. As a result of regular use in non-threatening situations these self-defense skills and strategies can be recalled and applied readily when our safety is threatened.

This concept of self-defense emphasizes prevention, avoidance, deterrence, and survival strategies. Techniques for escaping from an assailant are included but the primary goal is to eliminate the need for escape tactics and techniques. This book stresses the need for accurate information about assaults women commonly face, awareness of the environment around us through the use of our physical and intuitive senses, skills for appearing confident and assertive, and survival mechanisms. These important elements of self-defense are ones that can be incorporated into our daily lives.

Self-Care

As daughters, sisters, friends, partners, wives, mothers, aunts, and grandmothers, women are raised to nurture, help, take care of, and provide for the emotional and physical needs of others. In contrast, we have difficulty caring for and nurturing ourselves because we think it is selfish, conceited, arrogant, boastful, or vain. This conditioning can be deeply rooted.

For example, when a loved one, especially a child, is confronted with danger, women usually do not hesitate to intervene with actions that are quick-thinking, assertive, and physical. Women who think they could never yell will roar when a child is about to dart into traffic. Women who would never consider themselves athletic will dash and dart with blinding speed to save that child. Shy women, who shudder at the thought of drawing attention to themselves, will publicly make a scene for the safety of a child.

In a situation where the woman herself is in danger, she may worry about freezing in fear. She is often afraid of not being able to confront her attacker. Wondering whether she knows what to do, what other people will think, and if she can hurt or humiliate the assailant delays her responses. In contrast with protecting a child in danger, the possibility of over-reacting to the situation or causing a scene enters a woman's mind when she defends herself and limits her options.

The primary difference between the two responses above is whether a woman is defending herself or another person. Ultimately, self-defense is caring for our right to be safe and protecting that right with the same passion we feel when protecting the safety of others. It means working toward reacting to our own dangerous circumstances with the same certainty and confidence we used in situations when our children are in danger.

Women can care more about ourselves by affirming that because of who we are right now:

- we are worth defending,
- our safety is important,
- we will be missed if we are hurt or killed, and
- our contributions to the world, large or small, make it a better place.

Believing these things about ourselves can be difficult. Some of us may readily agree with them at first, but will have doubts upon introspection.

We live in a society which tolerates women being "put down". It is only beginning to value the contributions of women. This environment does not encourage us to consider our needs seriously. Most of us learn to care for others to the exclusion of our own need for care and appreciation.

Caring about ourselves is fundamental to self-defense because it motivates us to take action. When faced with danger, moving beyond fear and taking action to be safe requires incredible energy. As human animals, the survival instinct is often strong enough to produce action. Reinforcing this instinct with the conscious motivation that it is important for *me* to survive because of who *I* am generates actions which clearly demonstrate to assailants we will do everything possible to preserve our safety.

Improving Self-Care Skills

Thinking about caring for ourselves can bring up feelings of denial, guilt, indulgence, pain, emptiness, anger, anxiety, or frustration. The following ideas can help us better appreciate and care for ourselves on a day-to-day basis:

- Write down two things you like about yourself. These can be anything, large or small. The only rule is not to qualify them with wishes or negatives such as "I like that I am *generally* an organized person *but* when I'm stressed out, I *wish* I can be more in control." Instead, just write "I like that I am an organized person." Put this list where you will see it regularly. Add one more thing each month.

- As an introductory activity at a party or meeting, ask everyone to share two things they like about themselves.

- At the end of the day, think of at least one thing you did that you are *really* happy about. Keep a record of these things in a journal.

- Keep a list of things you like to do. These can be things that make you relax or laugh. You may like them because they help you feel good, contented, or inspired. Make time to do these things on a realistic, long-term basis. Turn to this list whenever you feel down, stressed, or depressed.

- As a game or exercise at a party or meeting, have everyone share two things they like about the person on their left (or right). Remember what was said about you.

- Accept a compliment without saying, "Thank you *but anyone could have done it,*" which discredits the compliment.

- Keep a journal of compliments given to you, no matter how trite they seem. Review it occasionally, especially when feeling down, stressed, or depressed.

- Develop a survival image. This is a mental picture, vision, or idea that gives you strength and motivates you to survive. It can be an image of you doing the things you enjoy most, someone you love, a tree, or a concept you cherish. It is whatever you value so much that nothing will force you to give it up. Reflect upon this image regularly, if only for a few minutes, when you feel safe and relaxed. Visualize it and project it through your face, speech, and actions to give you confidence and boost your morale.

Intuition

Caring for ourselves and our safety can prompt us to heighten our awareness of threats to our security. This awareness consists of observations made by the intuitive and physical senses. Intuitive messages play a special role in self-defense.

> A woman was invited by a male friend to hike to a waterfall she had always wanted to see. She had an uncomfortable feeling about this adventure but agreed to go because she really wanted to see the waterfall. When they arrived, the man expressed his real intentions. The woman escaped by making fun of his genitals and hiking out.

Intuition is a good tool for identifying assailants and situations that will become dangerous. It is very seldom wrong. Many survivors of assault say they felt some sort of intuitive danger signal before their assault began.

Women's intuition, however, is often ridiculed. Rational, linear thinking is valued by most people in this country more than knowledge acquired by means that are not so easily explained. However, countless women (and men) experience premonitions, gut feelings, flashes, hunches, or little voices which warn them about situations that could be dangerous, as in the true story above.

Using intuition means learning to identify and trust it, and then being willing to take action despite the possibility of embarrassment, over-reacting, or being wrong. (Avoiding assaults by expanding general awareness through our intuitive and physical senses will be discussed in more detail in Chapter 4.)

Choice

Every woman chooses for herself the options she will use in the situations she encounters. Options can be any action that makes a person feel safer from harassment, unwanted comments, touch, abuse, assault, or situations that make one incapable of informed consent regarding mutual activities like sex. Every option has worked well for someone, but not all options will work well for every person in every situation. The purpose of self-defense is to extend the range of options from which a person can choose. Each woman must then decide which options are appropriate depending on her situation, beliefs, skills, and intuitive messages.

People do the best they can in the situations they encounter. The number of options can seem to shrink or expand depending on a person's state of mind at the moment. No matter what the outcome of a woman's self-defense choices, her choice was the best one at the time and the only correct choice for her. She is never at fault for provoking or escalating an assault. The blame for an assault clearly rests on the assailant. No one ever has the right to abuse, hurt, take advantage of, or disregard the wishes of another person.

Submission as a defense option should never be interpreted as consent, which is an agreement freely made by all people involved and decided upon without intimidation. Women often choose to submit as the result of fear and coercion. Rather than indicating consent, submission is a strategy for survival.

People outside an assault situation often have opinions and judgments about what a woman being assaulted should do. Friends, relatives, police, and some self-defense instructors, even with the best intentions, will categorize responses as correct, stupid, and well- or ill-advised. These people, however, can never understand what the woman in the situation faced. Only the woman being assaulted can be aware of the details that influenced her decisions regarding her defensive actions. These details include her state of mind at the moment, her abilities and skills, and the intuitive messages she received. In addition, women being assaulted may not feel comfortable living with the consequences of actions advised by others.

The range of defense options is organized into the following categories, each covered in a separate chapter: prevention, avoidance, deterrence, escape, and survival. Important features of each category will be discussed. Skills and ideas for practicing them in non-threatening situations will be described. Specific options such as particular tactics and skill applications are listed in the Appendix.

Even though self-defense involves learning the facts regarding assault, knowing self-defense does not mean focusing on fear and danger. Self-defense uses information about assault to free women to live our lives with confidence and to improve our relationships with ourselves and others. As one woman said after completing a course based on this concept of self-defense:

> "I have gained confidence and awareness in almost all aspects of my life, not just dangerous situations, but in all relationships, and especially within myself."

2

SUCCESSFUL DEFENSE

A successful defense does not necessarily mean beating the attacker until he is completely incapacitated. It usually means surprising him with actions he does not expect, a story, or some other strategy that makes him hesitate just long enough for the defender to get away. Some women convince the assailants to flee. Persistence can play a major part in the success. Women often defend themselves successfully by listening to their intuition and then being assertive or changing their plans. Success can also mean surviving an assault and getting out of the situation alive.

The following true stories show how women can resist assaults successfully in many different ways. These are a small sampling of many, many instances of successful defenses:

- At a party, a woman met a man who shared her interest in aquariums. She accompanied him to his room to see his fish. When they entered, he kissed her, threw her on his bed, and was on top of her. She told him to get off. He said, "You didn't come here to look at the aquarium." She strongly repeated, "If you don't get off me, I'll scream." Finally, he said, "OK, get out."

- A woman who uses a wheelchair and recently had open heart surgery got rid of an intruder by giving him a well-placed, good, swift kick with one of her artificial legs.

- A woman with no phone lived on an isolated street with her abusive husband and decided to get help during a beating by running outside to a main street. People saw her husband beating her and stopped to help her escape.

- An elderly woman getting into her car was approached by a knife-wielding man wanting a ride. She refused, honked her car horn, and the man fled.

- After agreeing to dine at a restaurant with a male co-worker with whom she enjoyed many good conversational exchanges, a woman had a feeling that she shouldn't be alone with this man. She asked a female friend to accompany her when she canceled the date. The co-worker got very angry when he heard the news, screamed at them, and said he even cleaned his apartment and bought beer in preparation for the evening. The woman was glad she canceled the date because he had plans for much more than she had agreed to.

- Two six-year-old girls were approached by a group of teenage neighborhood boys the girls knew. One girl was held by two boys while a third boy kissed her. She bit down hard on the third boy's tongue and all three boys retreated. This girl then saw her friend held on the ground by several other boys. She ran hard and fast, right smack into the boys. Everyone fell over in a heap. She got up, grabbed her friend and together they ran to safety.

- A woman standing in a crowded subway was pinched on her behind by a stranger who then began to feel her. She lifted her arm high, pointed to the man, and loudly proclaimed, "This man is feeling my ass. I want him to stop." Unable to leave, everyone looked at the man, made fun of him, and voiced disapproval of his behavior.

- When a woman didn't want to have sex with her boyfriend of four years, he threw her forcefully onto the couch. Between the cushions, the woman found a fingernail file and jabbed it into his side. It felt like a knife. He became scared and left.

- At the end of a fun filled day of talking and activities, a woman went to a man's house for more conversation. They talked for a little while before he pushed the woman onto his bed for sex. She struggled verbally and physically. Unable to escape, she decided to pretend to submit. He sexually assaulted her. When he relaxed, she ran to safety.[1]

In contrast to these stories, women often grow up learning that defending themselves will cause greater injury, escalate an assault, and not be successful anyway. Television and movies support these ideas by portraying women as victims who struggle ineffectively and are unable to escape or stop their assaults. Women often believe that escaping successfully depends on the assistance of men. Those who do escape successfully on their own are usually labeled lucky.

News reports sensationalize brutal assaults on women and leave success stories on the back pages, if they are covered at all. Headlines usually read "Man With Knife Attacks Woman in Local Mall Parking Lot." This headline solicits fear, rather than spotlighting the woman's successful escape.

In addition, many success stories are never reported to the police, newspapers, or anyone. We can break this silence by sharing our own stories with others and listening to women talk about their experiences. In the process, we learn about the many instances in which women have escaped assault. This is an important step towards breaking down the beliefs many women are brought up with that undermine our ability to defend ourselves.

Re-Naming Our Experiences

Most women do not think they have self-defense successes until they are presented with examples, like the ones above, which demonstrate that self-defense is any strategy that increases one's safety. Once women acknowledge the many instances in which they successfully defend themselves, women who facilitate success story discussions have to conclude that successful resistance to assault is very common.

The following factors provide some explanations for the difficulty many women experience in recognizing their success in past experiences:

- All situations involving danger are traumatic, even when de-escalation or escape tactics are successful. This makes it easy to overlook or discredit the success-ful efforts.

- Many experiences may not seem like successes until the successful aspect is pointed out.

- Resistance is usually considered successful only when it makes the assailant completely helpless.

- Many instances of success are forgotten in the muddle of constant harassment, abuse and assault.

- Completed assaults can easily overshadow the success-ful instances of resistance and survival.

- Getting out of an uncomfortable situation that was not very threatening at the time may have thwarted a more dangerous assault had the situation continued.

- People talk so much about women being lucky when they resist assault that it is easy to believe one's own efforts involved luck rather than being important factors in the success.

- After a successful escape, it is common to theorize about what the assailant might have done. When these theories include situations that a woman feels incapable of escaping, she often concludes that luck was involved in the actual escape. In reality, the assailant did not follow through with any of the theoretical actions. The woman's resistance most likely had some effect on the assailant's decision to discontinue his assault, even though he "could" have done more. The woman should give herself credit for her escape.

Assault Resistance Research

Research does not support the common belief that women have few chances for successfully defending against assault. Several studies show that women who resist are often able to avoid rape.[2] One study found that:

- 81% who tried running were able to escape rape.
- 62.5% who screamed or yelled escaped successfully.
- 68% who used physical force of any kind avoided being raped.
- Outside intervention (or the threat of intervention) stopped a rape attempt in 83% of situations where it occurred.[3]

Intervention by people outside an assault situation has stopped many assaults. Although news accounts and women's stories sometimes describe instances when outside intervention failed to help the woman, assistance from others usually works because it increases the assailant's fear of getting caught. The situation also becomes more difficult for the assailant to control. Suggestions for involving outsiders, based on successful strategies women have used, are presented in Chapter 6.

Women who successfully resisted rape were more likely than those who did not resist successfully to be angered by the idea of being raped. These women were also more likely to be determined not to be raped. One researcher found that most women who successfully resisted rape did not perceive the situation as life threatening.[4] Another study found that women who successfully resisted felt less fear, helplessness, guilt, shock, and hurt during the assault.[5] In addition, women who escaped did not withdraw personally from the situation; there was no feeling that they weren't really there, it wasn't really happening to them, or they were outside their body watching the situation.[6]

Using a combination of strategies (for example: yelling, fighting, and running) was most likely to lead to escape from rape. In general, women who successfully resisted used physical force quickly, as soon as they perceived danger.[7] Another study supports the conclusion that immediate, aggressive action (fighting, yelling, running, verbal aggression) upon feeling fear or suspicion increased the likelihood of escape. It found that taking quick action means being willing to risk embarrassment and drawing attention to oneself.[8]

In order to act quickly, women may choose to risk overreacting and possibly misinterpreting the man's actions. Strong life-long messages for women not to hurt other people's feelings, especially those of acquaintances, make taking these risks difficult.

A different way to view this situation is to choose to value relationships with men who will respect a woman's willingness to protect her own safety. These men learn that actions which produce a defensive response by women can be interpreted as threatening and will take steps not to repeat them. Men who become angry or hurt by a woman's defensive response probably do not value the woman's desire to protect her safety. Perhaps it is time to re-evaluate relationships with these men.

Women are often discouraged from resisting assault because of beliefs that resistance will escalate the assault and result in greater injury, especially serious injury. Researchers, however, find that most women who resist rape are not seriously injured.

Except for their intention to rape, most rapists do not plan to cause other forms of injury.[9] Despite their threats of greater harm if women resist, rapists say they do not plan to carry out these threats.[10] Injuries are more likely to be caused by the assault and not the woman's resistance.[11] In one study, resistance was not linked to subsequent injury.[12] Deciding not to resist does not guarantee fewer injuries. One researcher, Pauline Bart, provides perspective on this issue. She finds that although there was a "somewhat higher possibility" of non-serious injuries for women who resisted, these women also had a "substantially higher probability of avoiding the rape."

The Successful Resister's Background

Bart's research into the childhood of women who successfully resist rape provides insight into family environments that can promote successful resistance skills when children become adults.[13] Her results do not create a formula which guarantees assault-free lives. Instead, they show how a woman's childhood socialization can affect her defense choices.

Women who avoided being raped were more likely to be raised with major household responsibilities. Their parents were less likely to intervene in sibling rivalries. Instead, parents encouraged their daughters to deal assertively with these conflicts. As children, these women imagined themselves participating in a workplace outside of the home. They were also more likely to have played contact sports like football.

As adults, Bart found these women more competent in managing stress and dealing with emergencies. Many were skilled in first aid, took self-defense classes, and participated in assertiveness training at some time in their lives. In addition, the women who avoided rape were "substantially more likely to engage in sports regularly."

These research findings are not meant to dictate correct responses to situations. Similarly, they do not imply that those without the described family environment or background are doomed to be assaulted. This information is presented to replace some of our fears and questions with facts. From it, people can make more informed choices about assault prevention planning, parenting, and lifestyle.

Most women have success stories to tell. These stories counter the notion that women do not and can not escape assault. By re-examining our experiences, we can re-name them as successes. Appreciating and giving ourselves credit for the times we stood up for ourselves can replace the tapes in our heads that say, "I can't," with ones that repeat "I'LL TRY, I CAN, and I HAVE TO because I AM WORTH IT."

3

PREVENTION: INFORMATION ABOUT ASSAULTS AGAINST WOMEN

The key to preventing assaults is having accurate information about who assailants are, why they assault women, and how assaults happen. Accurate information helps women identify situations that may lead to an assault and verifies intuitive messages that danger is present. This can help us be prepared to resist sooner in spite of the surprise and disorientation that usually occurs when faced with danger. Additional aspects of prevention are presented in "Self-Defense Options" in the Appendix.

The danger of being poorly informed is being surprised or taken off guard by an assailant. Accurate information can eliminate some of the confusion and disbelief common when an assault begins. Doubt can cause us to hesitate rather than react quickly to the danger. During this time, the assailant can increase his domination of the situation. The early, forceful resistance found to be successful for escape[14] may be delayed.

Because few assaults are reported, there are many misconceptions about assault.[15] The ones that are reported usually do not represent the types of assaults women commonly experience. News reports feature situations in which women are assaulted by strangers who use extreme violence and brutality. The entertainment media also depict these less common scenarios which seem impossible for women to escape.

Assailants, who are usually acquaintances, often convince women to believe they are alone in experiencing assault. Many assailants also try to convince the women they victimize that the violence they are experiencing is not really assault. These ideas that assailants attempt to convey to their victims block women from gaining an accurate picture of their experiences.

Historical Perspective

Women's daily struggles with violence and fear were different in the recent past than they are today in the U.S. Learning about the past can give us the courage to shape our future.[16]

Unlike today, wife abuse in the mid-1800s was so commonly acknowledged that illustrations of domestic violence were often found in mainstream publications. In 1875, The Woman's Journal began a weekly feature that listed specific incidences of wife abuse including beatings and murder.[17]

In the cities of the eighteenth and nineteenth centuries, women often helped each other deal with their abusive husbands. Neighborhood women intervened directly in family fights when necessary to provide individual women with the support and strength to struggle for their safety. They also organized public verbal confrontations of abusive men as a way to affect the business and social image of abusers.[18]

Things had changed by the 1930s. After World War I and the Depression, women's concerns regarding abuse were de-emphasized while the family unit was reinstated as an appealing symbol of harmony and stability. Society's perception of sexual abuse changed during this period. In the 1920s the problem "was moved from home to streets, the culprit transformed from father or other authoritarian male family member to perverted stranger, the victim transformed from innocent betrayed to sex delinquent."[19] This new view of sexual violence maintained the integrity of the family while pushing the reality of sexual assault and family violence underground.

With this new perception of sexual assault, domestic abuse and all violence against women became more hidden. The communication networks among women and neighborhood groups were dismantled. Women who were abused and assaulted were isolated once again. Public support for women victimized by domestic or sexual violence disappeared. By the 1970s, women felt so alone in their pain that many did not think anyone was abused except themselves. One woman remembers,

"I never talked to anyone. I never thought that any one else got hit. Nobody else had to hang up the phone when her husband came into the house. I was just very alone... This was my private responsibility."[20]

Times are changing again. Women are breaking the silence and talking about the violence they experience. Those who listen to women's stories are seeing patterns which contrast sharply with the ideas that the current society maintains about violence against women. The following information reflects these patterns.

It's Not the Psychotic Stranger

An important step to preventing assault is being able to identify, in advance, the people who are most likely to assault us. Many studies attempt to find demographic characteristics consistent among people who assault women.

In the reports studied, the assailants were all men. Researchers in separate studies of sexual and domestic violence were unable to find other characteristics, such as religion, family income, history of violence, past criminal record, or impulsive behavior, that would help identify assailants.[21] Except for the fact that most assailants are men, assailants have no other demographic characteristics in common.

Although it is known that some women are assaulted by other women, the evidence suggests that such incidences are very few.[22] Even in instances where men are raped, the assailants are almost always men. It is important to note that these assailants are not acting out homosexual tendencies. Instead, they are expressing power and control over other men in what they consider the most degrading manner, with sex. Researchers find that men who assault other men usually view themselves as heterosexual. They have and prefer heterosexual relationships.[23]

A Hard Look at Acquaintances

One factor, however, requires more serious attention. Most assailants know the women they victimize. The relationship can include brief encounters, acquaintances at work, authority figures, friends, and family.

A study of women who were raped or experienced attempted rape found that 89% were assaulted by someone they knew. One third of their assailants were dates, boyfriends, lovers, ex-lovers, husbands, or ex-husbands.[24] Research also finds that 99% of mentally and/or physically disabled people who are sexually abused are assaulted by friends, relatives, acquaintances, or caretakers of the victim.[25] In her book, I Never Called It Rape, Robin Warshaw provides an analogy which illustrates the prevalence of acquaintance rape: "Those figures [number of women sexually assaulted by someone they know] make acquaintance rape and date rape more common than left-handedness or heart attacks or alcoholism."[26]

Most rapes committed by acquaintances are not reported[27] because they do not resemble the conventional concept of rape which describes it as a violent and sudden act imposed by a stranger. Many women who survive acquaintance rape are afraid that their account of the rape will not be believed. Another difficulty in reporting acquaintance rape is that, due to the conventional concept of rape, it is often difficult to recognize these assaults as rape. The most difficult assaults to identify are ones in which the assailant had a close and intimate relationship with the woman.[28] Warshaw states, "For [the woman] to acknowledge her experience as rape would be to recognize the extent to which her trust was violated and her ability to control her own life destroyed."[29]

The difficult nature of acknowledging a situation as an assault can be a particular disadvantage in self-defense. Prompt identification of danger is necessary before the quick resistance that increases our chances for success[30] can begin. Knowing that assailants are usually acquaintances, identifying the men in our lives that make us uncomfortable, and setting our limits in situations that involve these men can help us recognize assaults quickly.

Among child victims of either gender, assaults by strangers are just as rare. Children and adolescents are sexually abused by someone they know up to 89% of the time. About one third of the abusers are related to the child.[31] One study concluded that the perpetrators of completed rapes against children were all relatives or acquaintances of the children.[32] The National Center for Missing and Exploited Children reported that only 2% of missing children were abducted by strangers. Most of the children were kidnapped by estranged parents or family acquaintances.[33] These figures demonstrate that children are much more at risk of assault by adults with whom they are familiar than by strangers.

Many women endure domestic violence, which is acquaintance assault by definition. It is estimated that a minimum of 30% of all wives in the U.S. experience physical aggression by their husbands.[34] Another study figures that 20% to 25% of all adult women in the U.S. have been physically abused at least once by men with whom they had intimate relationships. It also states that "battering may be the single most common source of serious injury to women, accounting for more injury than auto accidents, muggings, and rape combined."[35]

This violence spans a continuum of actions ranging from put-downs, insults, and threats to slapping, rape, and murder. Government statistics reveal that 30% of all female murder victims are killed by their husbands or boyfriends.[36]

The high percentage of women who are raped by someone they know, the majority of child assaults and abductions committed by adults familiar with the child, and the violence women experience within domestic relationships make it clear that almost all assaults women and children face involve acquaintances as assailants. This means the men most likely to assault us will have the demographic characteristics such as age, race, economic background, profession, religion, size, and psychological profile of the men with whom we normally associate. It also means retraining our minds to associate assailants with acquaintances rather than strangers when reading or talking about men who assault women.

We can identify the men who are most likely to assault us by listening to intuitive messages and watching for behavioral clues from the individual men with whom we have contact. By making safety plans for situations that involve men who could be safety threats or who we know will assault us, we can avoid confrontations that may escalate to assault. Chapter 4 will describe the role of intuitive messages and behavioral clues in identifying possible assailants. Safety planning guidelines are described in the Appendix.

Why Do Men Assault Women?

Understanding the motivation that causes men to assault women helps us analyze the strengths and weaknesses of our assailants. This information is an important aspect of safety planning because it helps us prepare realistic defense strategies, including those which avoid, deter, and help women escape assault.

The primary motivation for men to abuse, batter, and assault women is to express power, domination, and control.[37] It is difficult to explain why the need to express these things becomes manifested in violence for some men.[38] One explanation for rape involves the link between sex and aggression with masculinity. Men who see rape as "aggressive sex" may view rape as an acceptable form of masculine behavior.[39] In a study that interviewed rapists, none stated that a lack of sexual outlet was the reason for their rapes.[40] These findings show that the belief that men rape women primarily for sexual gratification is a myth.

Expectations placed on men in this society can easily lead to feelings of general inadequacy. Social pressure to be the family provider and protector, a strong leader, and in control of emotions can lead to goals which are unrealistic, unattainable and unwanted. The frustration resulting from not being able to meet expectations can lead to violent and abusive behavior.[41]

Some men learn to use violence to express their anger and frustration from the family violence they experienced as children. Although not all men who witness domestic abuse or experience sexual assault as children become assailants, solving problems through violence is modeled for children who grow up in abusive families.[42] Children often have few other resources for learning communication, anger control, and problem-solving skills.

Men are likely to feel sexually inadequate in a society that stresses male sexual superiority and conquest through the glorification of James Bond-type characters and music idols who model sexually aggressive behavior. The pressure from peers to match the sexual accomplishments of these models of male sexuality will inevitably make many men fall short of their unrealistic and elusive goals.[43] It is perhaps this level of sexual inadequacy which leads so many men to use sex as the means to express power, domination, and control through rape. Despite societal pressures, however, men are still responsible for their own actions and can choose not to abuse women.

In dating situations, a sexual attraction may exist and be the basis for initiating intimacy. The motivation, however, is no longer sexual when the assailant fails to respect his partner's sexual boundaries and/or disregards her request to stop. Any time a woman feels a loss of control in the situation, she may feel assaulted or raped.

Assailants do not want to get caught. Most are not looking for a fight. A fight can attract the attention of outsiders as well as put the assailant at risk of injury. Instead, assailants are looking for easy and safe situations to assert dominance and control. This information can help women develop successful avoidance, deterrence, and resistance strategies.

Violence is Not News to Women

In any group of three or more women, *at least one* will be a survivor of assault.[44] This conclusion is based on many statistics which attempt to quantify women's experiences with violence. When researching assault rates, consideration must be given to the fact that few assaults are reported to anyone.[45] Many women do not identify their victimization as assault, making their reports non-existent.[46] One study found the rate of rapes committed to be ten to fifteen times greater than rates based on the official National Crime Survey.[47]

Because women in this society are generally perceived as passive, weak, and submissive, no groups of women are exempt from being targeted for assault. There are no significant differences in age, education, and ethnicity between women who were raped and those who have not been raped.[48] Another study found no differences in family income, religion, or the size of the city where women who have been assaulted lived compared to women who have not been assaulted.[49] The primary motivation behind rape is not sex, but is instead, to overcome a sense of inadequacy by asserting power, dominance, and control. Therefore, sexual unavailability due to age, looks, marriage, or being a mother is no guarantee of safety.

Some women are also members of other groups that are generally perceived in this society as exploitable or vulnerable. As a result of additional discrimination and oppression, some of these women are targeted more frequently in assaults. Many assaults will involve authority figures or caretakers as assailants. Some people are victims of social myths which can provoke others to be violent against them. These groups include children and young people, both girls and boys, elderly people, people of color, lesbians, new immigrants, un-documented residents, and people with physical or mental disabilities. There are additional safety risks for those who are fat or small in stature, and who have difficulty speaking English.

These people communicate, perceive the environment, and understand the world differently from adults in the dominant culture. Their interpretation of behaviors and body language, use of personal space, and physical abilities can affect their awareness of possible assault, increase their vulnerability, and reduce the number of defensive options available. Considering these differences is an important part of safety planning.

Many of us would prefer to hold on to society's myths which identify other women as the ones who face assault rather than ourselves. In addition to providing a false sense of security, believing that violence is imposed on other women can make quick defensive action difficult when we are confronted with assault. It also wrongly emphasizes a woman's appearance and behavior as an explanation for her victimization. This emphasis perpetuates another myth: that the woman is, at least partially, to blame for her assault.

This information is not presented to scare women, although it can be quite frightening. Its purpose is to help women recognize the reality of violence and work toward eliminating the myths we were taught. Using accurate information about assault to create safety strategies is an important step in taking control of our lives.

Beware of the Streets at Night!

This warning is said and heard so often that women sometimes become fearful even during walks on well-lit streets with no signs of danger. Data from rape crisis centers show that instead of occurring outdoors, 64% of all sexual assaults occurred in the victim's or the assailant's home. Another 11% of assaults took place in other homes, buildings, or at the workplace. Only 16% of assaults were committed outdoors. Almost all children and elderly people are assaulted indoors.[50] In a study on date rape, 85% occurred in the victim's or the assailant's home while only 4% took place outdoors.[51]

Fear of the street at night is usually associated with attacks committed by strangers. As stated earlier in this chapter, strangers are much less likely to be assailants than acquaintances.[52] Since most people see acquaintances indoors where they live, work, study, socialize, and shop, it makes sense that most assaults occur in those locations. In addition, assailants may feel less risk of getting caught and more control over their environment inside locked rooms. Outdoors, passersby may witness the assault and intervene.[53]

Changing Our Images of Assault

In contrast to many people's image of assault, half of all rapes begin with ten minutes of casual conversation in a safe, public place. During these ten minutes, the assailant assesses his chances of easily carrying out his plans and begins to set the process of dominance in motion.[54] He may do this by asking questions, touching the woman, trying to move the situation to a more private location, or using threats to test the woman's determination to assert her right to safety. This is also the time when women receive intuitive and behavioral clues warning of danger. It is so early in the assault that avoidance and de-escalation strategies are commonly successful.

Many assaults begin and end quickly. Others last for hours or days. Some are very physically violent with bruises, torn clothing, and broken furniture as evidence. The amount of physical force does not characterize the seriousness of the situation. Coercion through verbal threats can be as terrifying as physical violence. Some assailants use a trick or ploy to entice a child or to gain a woman's confidence. The ploy can extend over time into a relationship in which the assailant feels he has total control. This is common in child assaults and domestic violence. Many assaults, especially domestic battering situations, often follow a pattern that is identifiable and repeated.

People often have a set image of how assaults take place. In reality, assailants initiate and escalate their assaults in many different ways. Loosening rigid notions of how assaults occur is one way to prepare for anything that might happen and decrease the chance that surprise will negatively affect our reaction time.

Weapons: Fear Versus Fact

Many women's biggest fear is facing an armed attacker. Fear of death is a common response. Assaults that make the news and are portrayed in the entertainment media often fuel these fears. Many women have been hurt by weapons, but in the overwhelming majority of assaults no weapon of any kind is present. In addition, most people injured by weapons do not die.

The following statistics regarding weapon use by assailants together with the high probability of surviving weapon wounds can greatly affect a woman's choice to resist.[55]

- In 93% of all rapes, no guns were present.

- Another study which investigated the presence of all weapons found that in 75% of all rapes, no weapons of any kind were involved.[56]

- Only about 1% of all crimes that involved handguns resulted in fatalities.

- Of the 99% of all violent crimes involving handguns where there were no fatalities, 85% of the victims were not injured, 10% received minor injuries, and only 2% were shot. Of those who were shot, only 21% were hospitalized for three or more weeks.

- Women were less than half as likely to encounter a handgun in an attack as men.

- City dwellers were a little more than twice as likely to be victimized in a crime with a handgun present than people living in the suburbs. These suburban inhabitants faced crimes involving handguns about one and one half times more often than rural residents.

- Guns and knives appear to be used to coerce a victim into meeting demands rather than to injure the victim. When guns were present 49% of rapes were completed. 42% of rapes with knives present were completed. In contrast, only 28% of rapes were completed when no weapon was used.[57]

- Of all non-fatal crimes involving assailants with handguns, 87% of the guns were never fired, 10% were discharged but missed the victim, and only 2% of all these crime victims were wounded. The study researching the presence of all weapons[58] found that in 78% of all assaults involving assailants with knives, the knives were never used. Attempted stabbings were reported in 12% of all the assaults where knives were present with only 10% of all assailants stabbing their victims.

- Victims were more likely to face armed assailants if they were strangers. Weapons were used in 68% of stranger assaults while only 26% of acquaintance assaults and 6% of assaults where assailants were relatives included weapons.[59]

- Robberies were more than twice as likely to involve assailants with guns than rape or other assaults. Guns were present in 18% of the robberies, 7% of rapes, and 8% of all other assaults.

The low percentage of rapes involving assailants with weapons, the low incidence of injury when faced with armed assailants, and the very small proportion of victims shot by assailants carrying guns is surprising to many. It appears that although women do experience armed assaults, the frequency is much lower than many women are led to believe.

Weapon use may be so infrequent because of the high incidence of assaults committed against women by acquaintances rather than strangers. In addition, since women are generally perceived as weak and submissive, assailants may believe that women can be intimidated without the use of weapons.

Many people believe that a knife attack or gun shot will lead to death. In fact, most people survive both knife and gun wounds. Many knife wounds are not severe. They can be like the accidental cuts people experience which heal with time. Most gun wounds are more severe but not lethal. People who are shot usually recover with appropriate medical attention.

A belief that gun shots are fatal, on the other hand, can affect survival. People receiving wounds that are not usually lethal have died because their fear of death might have led to shock and other complications. Knowing that gun shots are survivable can minimize fear. This is another example of how accurate information can increase the likelihood of surviving assaults.

How to Identify an Assault Myth

The following is a summary of common beliefs about assaults against women which are false. They are myths which must be replaced by facts as summarized above. The notes at the end of this book and the bibliography in the Appendix are provided as resources for more detailed information.

- A woman's looks, actions, or reputation are responsible for, cause, or promote the assault or escalation of the assault in some way.

- Some women like or want to be assaulted.

- Some women are safe from assault.

- Women can be absolutely assured of safety in specific situations.

- Women and children do not tell the truth during an assault or in their accounts of it afterward.

- Women must accept a certain amount of risk when they participate in certain activities.

- Women, especially those who are young, elderly, or disabled, are incapable of resisting assault.

- Assailants always escalate their assaults, inflict serious injury, and become more enraged when women resist them.

- Involving others (or any other resistance option) is not a successful defense strategy.

- Most women are lucky when they successfully resist assault.

- Resisting an assailant who has a weapon will result in certain death.

- Certain types of men are more likely to be abusers or assailants than others.

- Men can not control themselves, especially sexually, in certain situations.

- Men who assault children or other men are expressing their sexual preference.

- Assaults usually occur in situations that will most likely involve strangers.

- It is reasonable for men to abuse or assault other people in certain circumstances or for certain reasons.

- Assaults always follow certain simple formulas or have certain components.

- Some assaults should be taken more seriously than others.

- Sexual and domestic violence are not common, especially among certain groups of people.

An understanding of women's most common experiences with violence can help all women make informed self-defense decisions. Strategies can be based on what is most likely to happen rather than our worst fears which may be less common. Although facing an assault will always be terrifying, we will be more prepared and less surprised. This increases our chances of successfully avoiding or resisting assault.

4

AVOIDANCE:
AWARENESS WITH ALL OUR SENSES

Avoiding assault altogether is the preferred choice of most women. It means perceiving an impending assault and taking steps to keep that assault from occurring. The assailant has not yet begun to assert his dominance. Avoidance is based on an awareness of intuitive messages and observations of our physical surroundings, including the behavior of others, that warn us of danger. A heightened awareness helps us identify:

- people who may test, hurt, assault, or assist us
- situations that may be dangerous or escalate into violence
- defense options to choose in particular situations if they become necessary
- the little and great things that make life beautiful and interesting

Many think of avoidance as imprisoning themselves in their homes. Although home security is important, it is not the only, nor necessarily the best method since much abuse and violence occurs in the home. In addition, this method limits women's actions. Avoidance strategies which rely on awareness can free women from such limitations while taking steps to avoid danger.

Being aware of the environment around us requires the use of all our physical and intuitive senses. Knowing which senses are stronger, more developed, and, therefore, most useful allows us to analyze our advantages and disadvantages. We can work to strengthen the senses which are strong or well developed and, when possible, improve the senses that are more limited.

Improving awareness through intuition and observation will be described in this chapter. Actions that can keep assaults from occurring use awareness in combination with the facts about assault examined in the previous chapter. These tactics are described in "Self-Defense Options" in the Appendix.

Identifying Potential Assailants

Recognizing that assailants are usually acquaintances can be an advantage. People we meet and know often evoke impressions ranging from *nice person* and *someone to learn from* to *be careful, jerk,* and general discomfort. Children often have very clear impressions of others. A negative impression is one way that our intuition can warn us of the possibility that this person will disrespect, abuse, or assault us.

Listening to these warnings and making safety plans based on these intuitive messages does not have to prevent us from developing working relationships with those who produce these negative feelings. For example, we may decide that saying hello or participating in social functions with a neighbor who makes us uncomfortable is acceptable. Meanwhile, we might also set limits that forbid this neighbor from entering our homes and require that we are never alone with him. Taking these impressions seriously is a way to be cautious and avoid situations that can escalate into undesirable ones.

Observations of behavior can also help us identify those who might abuse or assault us. In the book, I Never Called It Rape,[60] Robin Warshaw lists behaviors that can warn women about men who might be assailants. Taken individually, some of these behaviors do not constitute abuse or assault but people who exhibit several of them may be showing a pattern that can lead to violence. A woman may decide to take precautions and make safety plans when she is around people who exhibit one or more of the following behaviors:

- Emotional abuse: insulting or belittling comments, ignoring other's opinions
- Negative talk about women in general, people of color, people with disabilities
- Jealousy for no reason
- Drug or heavy alcohol use, tries to intoxicate others
- Agitation in response to a companion's decision not to get drunk, have sex, or accompany him to his room or apartment
- Wanting control over many elements of another's life: how to dress, who friends should be, which movie to see or restaurant to patronize
- Anger about sharing the expenses of a date
- Grabbing, pushing, or other physically violent behavior
- Actions that intimidate: sitting too close, blocking your way with his body, speaking like he knows you better than he does, touching you without permission, kicking chairs or trash cans
- Anger when unable to handle sexual and emotional problems
- Acting smarter than or socially superior to others
- A fascination with weapons

- Cruelty exhibited to animals, children, or people he can bully

It is unfortunate, but necessary, that women and children must think about their safety around people they know. Given the prevalence of abuse and assault committed by acquaintances, unconditionally trusting any group of people is unsafe. Decisions about who and when to trust must be made on an individual basis by using intuitive clues and behavioral observations.

Identifying Potentially Dangerous Situations

Most assaults against women begin with a testing period when an assailant, consciously or not, assesses his chances of successfully carrying out his plans through conversation or attempts at domination. During this period, women often pick up clues that the situation may become abusive or violent based on intuition and/or the potential assailant's behavior.

In domestic assaults and assaults against children, this testing period can extend over time, sometimes lasting for years. The assailant uses this time to manipulate his victim with threats, bribes, and secrets. The manipulations may not appear abusive when viewed as individual incidents but the assailant uses them to increase his control of the relationship until he has obtained dominance. Intuitive messages can provide warnings that this process is beginning.

Children are often unable to articulate their feelings or verbally identify how they are being manipulated. One way to help children express their intuitive feelings about confusing or potentially dangerous situations is to describe these as "uh-oh feelings." Encourage them to talk to others, especially adults they feel comfortable with, whenever they feel that "uh-oh." Children often feel more comfortable talking to adults about these things when they are discussed in he context of safety such as fire and crossing streets, are assured they will be taken seriously, and know that everything possible will be done to protect them. Women and children who identify potential assaults have used many different strategies to try avoiding them. Showing confidence, communicating assertively, being unwilling to let potential assailants control their location or activities, and changing the situation by leaving or inviting others to join it are strategies that are often successful. Confident and assertive communications are discussed in Chapter 5.

Women have also had intuitive premonitions of sudden assaults which occur without this testing period. In situations that would otherwise be normal, they felt a distinct sense of fear or foreboding. Because it was unexplainable, some discounted the intuitive warning and had to try deterring or escaping the assault. For those who heeded the warning and avoided the situation, most may never know if an assault would have occurred.[61] The fact that they took action to be safe and there was no assault means that they have a success story to tell.

Embracing Intuition

By trusting our intuition, most assaults can be avoided before a confrontation begins. Intuition is a very powerful self-defense tool because it is a reliable indicator of safety and danger which most women and children possess. Intuition increases general awareness by adding information which one senses to the facts received through physical perception.

A little voice, tug, flash, tightness in the stomach, feeling of dread, gut feeling, "uh-oh" feeling, sudden enlightenment, hunch, premonition... People perceive intuitive thoughts in different ways. These thoughts are not derived from logical, rational, analytical reasoning. They seem to be unquestionably true but are not easy to explain. Unlike emotions, intuitive feelings can be easily ignored. People often overlook them because it is easy to assume that if there is no physical reason behind something, it can not really be true.[62]

Many women learn or feel pressure to ignore intuitive feelings. Women's intuition is often ridiculed. Negative thoughts or impressions about others are often suppressed because many women are taught to value the feelings of others above our own. We often perceive these thoughts as being hurtful to others rather than as warning signs for us. In this way, intuitive feelings that can help us avoid assault are not taken seriously.

Intuition can both supplement and substitute for the physical senses. Those of us whose physical senses are restricted by blindness, deafness, movement limitations, or other disability might find intuition a major source of information about the environment. Identifying intuitive messages and developing our intuitive abilities are skills that most people can improve with practice.

Intuitive messages and rational thinking work together to help women avoid assault. Each can verify the other. For example, an intuitive message of danger is less likely to be discounted if the situation the message refers to is compatible with the facts of assault presented in the Chapter 3.

Confusing Messages

Intuition used in assault avoidance can become confused with fear. Fear based on truly intuitive feelings is a warning that signals a need to make safety decisions. In contrast, fear can seem to be the result of an intuitive message but actually be prompted by lack of confidence, myths about assault, media attention on assault, and prejudice rather than intuition.

Danger can seem to lurk behind every dark corner outside at night. Every stranger can seem more evil than the last. These fears are spread by myths about assault which most people grow up with. A lack of confidence can make many situations seem scarier than they really are. Knowing about women's most common experiences with assault can balance these fears with rational thought.

Attention on local assaults often produces general fear and paranoia. When the assailant has identifiable physical characteristics like skin color, dialect, and size, this fear can spread to an uneasiness about all people who share the physical characteristics of the assailant. Precautions are appropriate if an individual exhibits most aspects of the description of an assailant at large. Fear based solely on a physical characteristic, however, is common and prejudicial. A persons color, size, dialect, or disability are often cited as reasons for feeling uncomfortable about an individual. These factors, however, do not make a situation unsafe.

It is usually a person's behavior, overt or subtle, that influences our intuitive feelings regarding safety. Being uncomfortable primarily because of a person's physical characteristics is based on prejudice. Prejudice creates a fear that is based on who a person is rather than what the person does.

True intuition is seldom wrong. Trying to separate the fears that intuition produces from the fear that is influenced by other factors can help determine the urgency for implementing protective measures. Keeping in mind the factors that can pass for intuition, women can learn to identify truly intuitive messages more accurately and use them in ways that enhance our safety.

Strengthening Our Intuitive Powers

Two steps for improving our intuition are first to value it, then to become more aware of it. Valuing our intuition can be difficult in a society that appreciates rational, analytical thought more highly.

An accurate analytical method of identifying assailants and situations that might escalate into violence has yet to be found. The intuitive method, although anecdotal, has worked well for many women. For our safety's sake, we can learn to value intuition. Once we believe in its importance, we can open ourselves to its possibilities, test it, and see its potential.

Accurate identification of intuitive messages begins by learning that they usually:

- are sensed, rather than being a thought or emotion
- are not the product of rational thought
- make us feel quite certain they are true
- induce fear, rather than being caused by fear

Having many extraneous thoughts and emotions can obstruct the perception of intuitive messages. A relaxed, calm mind focussed on the present is conducive to sensing intuitive feelings. Becoming more aware of how intuitive messages are received and what they feel like for each of us can make them easier to recognize.

The following are some ideas for becoming more aware of intuitive messages and how they affect our lives:

- Observe people working, learning, shopping, eating, relaxing. Notice your reactions to them. Identify these as intuitive, judgmental, emotional, rational, or prejudicial.

- Observe how your body normally feels inside: facial muscles, jaw, neck and shoulders, chest, stomach. Many people perceive intuitive messages through subtle changes in these places. Being more aware of how our bodies normally feel helps identify changes that signify an intuitive message.

- We usually know when we are too close to another person but we don't usually think about how we know it. Notice the distance you set between yourself and others. Try to figure out how that distance was set.

- Notice how intuition is used to decide the right time to ask someone for help or a favor.

- Intuition often helps inspire ideas. Analyze how you get good ideas and where intuition plays a part.

- Sometimes a behavior, like running, swimming, or talking to someone, will stimulate intuitive ideas. Identify the behavior that helps you receive intuitive messages and use it to generate new intuitive ideas.

- Analyze the mix of emotions, logic, and intuitive hunches or "tugs" that are involved in making decisions.

- People who have difficulty finding intuition within themselves might be aided by observing how others are intuitive. Try using others as models for stimulating your own intuition.

- Keep a record of the situations when intuition was perceived and used. Including many details in the description of the intuitive messages makes future recognition of these messages easier.

Testing our intuition can increase our awareness of it as well as increase our trust in it. Be aware of situations where intuition can be used and verified. For example, try to sense where your parking space will be in a large, crowded parking lot. People who sell things to the public can try intuitively identifying a shopper who will buy their product. Verify your intuition by observing the shopper or approaching the shopper with your sales pitch. Use the record of your intuition suggested above to verify hunches and premonitions.

Expanding the meaning of awareness to include the intuitive dimension as well as the physical senses can enhance our everyday lives. It can increase our general awareness of the people and environment around us so we can appreciate the details, changes, and events of our world that may otherwise go unnoticed. Trusting and strengthening our intuitive potential improves our creativity, problem-solving skills, and decision making abilities while helping us identify warnings that signal danger. Testimonials from many women about intuitive warnings reveal intuition as one aspect of awareness that can not be ignored.

5

DETERRENCE:
CONFIDENCE AND ASSERTIVENESS

The assailant has begun the process of asserting his dominance. He may try to control the situation verbally with threats, bribes, insults, or general harassment. He may also be physically threatening or attempt to move the situation to a more isolated and sheltered location.

Deterrence options keep the assailant from escalating his violence so that the assault does not progress. An important factor in deterrence is confident and assertive behavior.

Appearing confident and assertive are effective tactics of self-defense. They are often used successfully and are practical in all stages of assault. In addition to keeping assaults from escalating, women have used confident and assertive behavior to avoid assaults before they began and to escape once assaults are initiated. Portraying confidence and assertiveness can be especially useful for children and people who have difficulty using fighting skills.

Examples of tactics using behaviors that communicate confidence and assertiveness are listed in "Self-Defense Options" in the Appendix.

Many women want to learn confidence and assertiveness skills for their other benefits. These skills can be used to improve relationships within families, among friends, and in the workplace. Many women report improved self-esteem when they are able to express their needs in ways that feel appropriate.

It is often difficult, however, for women to appear confident and assertive. The following comments explain some of the reasons confidence and assertiveness are a challenge for many women:

- I have a hard time saying what I mean.
- When I feel vulnerable, I don't know what to say.
- I need to think about speaking up more.
- All my life I've been told that speaking up for myself is not lady-like.
- The hardest thing for me is to be assertive with people I am close to.
- In the situations I'm afraid of, I feel I can't say anything because there is so much to lose, like my job.
- I worry that I'll hurt the other person's feelings.
- Looking people in the eye really feels uncomfortable, especially when the situation is tense.
- When I'm afraid, I just want to hide.

In spite of the difficulties, many women have successfully deterred assailants by appearing confident and assertive in situations that were threatening. Confidence and assertiveness can keep many situations from becoming ones where escape measures become necessary.

Expressing Determination Deters Assault

Our determination to protect ourselves is a message potential assailants receive in the way we communicate. In addition to the actual words we speak, much is expressed by the way our bodies are held, the expression on our faces, and the way our words are said. When these components of communication all say the same thing, the message becomes very strong and clear.

As described in Chapter 3, assailants often assess their chances of being able to carry out their assaults in a testing period. Research confirms that assertive body language is a factor leading to the "elimination of prospective victims" by assailants.[63] Since most assailants are looking for an easy and safe situation to assert dominance and control, assaults often do not occur when the woman is perceived to be assertive, confident, unwilling to be overpowered, and determined to protect her safety.

Portraying Confidence

The goal of using confidence as a self-defense tool is to be perceived by others as a confident person. Conveying an image of confidence can be achieved rather easily and will be described in the following pages. Learning to actually feel confident, especially in threatening situations, is often a longer, more difficult process. However, using and practicing the skills of conveying a confident image puts in motion the process of becoming a confident person.

Checklist for Confident Body Posture

Much of what we say is communicated by the way we hold our bodies. The following is a checklist of physical positions which creates a posture that projects confidence, whether or not we actually feel confident. Practicing this posture by applying it in many everyday situations will usually improve a person's feeling of confidence.

- feet flat on the floor, shoulder width apart
- knees slightly bent
- chest lifted
- shoulders back
- arms hanging loosely by your side
- continuous relaxed breathing
- head lifted
- eye contact. Look at the forehead or nose if looking at eyes is difficult.

This posture physically helps keep our minds from going blank and our bodies from freezing. It ensures a continuous flow of blood and oxygen to the entire body, especially the brain, when we are afraid or nervous. With our heads lifted, we can see and hear better, improving general awareness. In this position, others can not see the sweating palms, pounding heart, or knotted stomach that fear or lack of confidence produces. Instead, other people see a woman in a strong but neutral position communicating confidence and control.

When standing is not appropriate or possible, most of the checklist can still apply. To appear confident when sitting, place the legs next to each other with both

(right) People react to the image they see. Uneven weight distribution, slouching posture, a retreating personal space, and downcast eyes not only communicate hesitancy and passivity, they make awareness and resistance difficult.

feet flat on the floor if possible. Avoid fidgeting with the hands, hiding them in pockets, or crossing them. Keep arms hanging loosely at the side and hands on the lap, chair arms, or table. The upper body can be straight or slightly leaning forward.

Eye contact conveys different messages in different cultures. It is considered confident in most of the United States but it can be perceived as a threat or considered rude in other countries. Even in the streets of some large American cities, an unwritten rule exists: Do not look a stranger in the eye because it is considered an invitation to fight. When planning to be with people different from ourselves, observing and asking about the meaning of eye contact and other physical gestures can avoid problems.

Practice using this checklist during ordinary interactions with others. Begin with easy situations and progress to ones that are more stressful, risky, and/or confrontational. Notice how others react to you. Notice how you feel when you use this posture. Compare this to how you feel when you do not use it. Notice the posture of others and how you and other people react to them.

(right) The woman with a confident body posture has a good chance of deterring an assault, even if she feels afraid and uncertain.

Facial Expression

The determination behind a person's words is often visible in the facial expression. Humor, anger, fear, and conviction can be seen in a person's forehead, eyes, mouth, and jaw. People are not usually taken seriously when their facial features do not match what is being said, such as telling an aggressor to stop while grinning widely. Practice assertive strategies while watching yourself in the mirror. Try to correct facial expressions that do not match what is being said.

Voice

Another indicator of confidence is how the voice sounds. Some voices sound meek and passive. Any voice, including a soft one, can be very powerful when accompanied by strong eye contact and body language. People often perceive loud voices as boisterous and aggressive. Statements that begin at an appropriate loudness but end softly are often not taken seriously. A voice that is steady and appropriately loud usually sounds confident and communicates a commitment to the message.

Personal Space

Controlling personal space is an abstract but effective strategy for portraying confidence. People usually think they see a confident person when the individual's personal space does not retreat or shrink when confronted, nervous, or afraid. For abuse or assault to occur, the assailant must verbally or physically disregard, step into, invade, or shrink our personal space. When personal space is perceived as large and well protected, people tend to respect it. When it is expanded, the range of our physical and intuitive senses can expand with it, enlarging our awareness.

Our bodies take up physical space. Personal space is the area around our bodies which is also claimed as our own. We are aware of and have control over what it contains and what occurs inside.

Certain people, such as loved ones and children, are often allowed inside, but when others step in we may feel uncomfortable, crowded, or invaded.

Personal space roughly encloses a cylindrical area the length of the body with a diameter defined by outreached arms. Some people feel their space invaded when they can no longer see an approaching person's feet in their peripheral vision while maintaining eye contact. Personal space can expand or shrink depending on one's confidence, self-esteem, mood, or skill in manipulating it.

Learning to control our personal space begins with observations. Try to see and feel the boundaries of your space in daily activities and in regular interactions with people. Notice how and when those boundaries change. Expanding personal space can feel like "sending out vibes" or "puffing up". When it shrinks, it can feel crowded or cozy.

Observe your reactions to other people's personal boundaries. One person may invite a hug nonverbally, allowing you to enter her personal space. For others, you may get the feeling that it is not the right time to enter the room they occupy because their space has filled the entire area.

In a situation where your boundaries seem to be naturally expanding, try making them expand farther. Another approach for making your space expand is to identify the factors that contribute to your space expanding. Visualize those factors being in place, get in touch with how you feel when your personal space naturally expands, and will your personal space to enlarge. Experiment in safe non-threatening situations where the probability for success is high.

Expand your personal space, use the checklist for confident body posture, match your facial expression with the intended message, and speak with a steady, clear voice for an unquestionably confident image. Try this while walking down the hall or street, standing in line at the grocery store, talking to a doctor, or participating in a meeting. Watch people's reactions. Women have shared stories about people on the sidewalk moving out of their way, men saying "Good Morning" instead of shouting their usual insults, and finally feeling some respect from others when they use these skills.

Becoming aware of and learning to control personal space can be enhanced with visualizations. Try the following when you feel relaxed, calm, and safe:

> Imagine a safe, protected place. Be in it. Feel with all your body what it is like to be truly safe. Let this sensation fill your entire being and personal space. Now, enclose it all in a secure bubble of protection. You and your personal space fill this bubble. You can expand it or shrink it at will. Try it. See yourself in your life protected by this bubble. You choose who and what can enter it and under what circumstances. Other people can see it and know that it must be respected. Within this bubble, you are protected from abuse, assault, and violence. When violence stands outside it, the bubble releases your courage, confidence, and strength. Feel the safety of the bubble, remember how it feels, and think of the bubble whenever you feel afraid.

Communicating with Assertive Behavior

One way to recognize assertive behavior is to compare its characteristics with the features of passivity and aggressiveness. The following lists of passive, aggressive, and assertive characteristics can help us understand the differences among these behaviors.

Signs of passive behavior are:[64]

• making excuses

• being apologetic

• speaking in a voice that is hard to hear

• blaming yourself when things go wrong

• looking down or away

- answering questions that you do not want or do not need to answer
- not claiming your opinions; saying: "Don't you really mean ...?" which allows the other person to claim your opinion, instead of: "I think ...."
- not saying what is really felt
- giving up personal space by backing up, leaning backward, flinching, or shrinking the body

Passive behavior often communicates to potential assailants a lack of determination to assert one's unwillingness to go along with an attack. People can often find ways to continue conversations with a person who is showing passive behavior when she actually wants it to stop. Continually finding excuses and answering questions can also be frustrating when being passive.

Aggressive behavior is often identified by:

- loud voice
- name-calling or swearing
- accusations, especially those based on assumptions and judgments
- rough touch or other physically inappropriate behavior
- invading the personal space of others by advancing and stepping into it
- not allowing others to express themselves
- disregard for the needs and feelings of others
- threats and intimidation
- humiliation

Some people are offended or feel challenged by aggressive behavior and may react by escalating their violence. Others feel over-powered when a person responds to them aggressively. They may also fear the attention an aggressive response causes and will stop or leave the situation. Aggressive people communicate to others their willingness to do anything, even things not usually considered appropriate.

In a self-defense context, aggressive behavior can be considered appropriate and necessary in some circumstances. It can be useful for de-escalating or escaping an assault. Using aggressive behavior often threatens the assailant with outside intervention which can persuade him to stop his violence. Based on the judgment of the woman involved, potential danger may dictate doing whatever is needed to de-escalate the situation or escape.

Being assertive generally means taking action that communicates our needs, desires, feelings, opinions, and rights without being abused or taken advantage of. These actions also do not abuse or take advantage of others.[65] Assertive behavior is characterized by:

- honesty
- self-respect
- clear and direct communication of feelings and opinions
- comments on observations of behavior rather than attacks or conclusions about the person
- descriptions rather than judgements
- an exploration of alternatives rather than providing solutions or advice
- some risk taking
- a steady voice loud enough to be heard
- direct eye contact
- voice, words, body posture, and facial expressions all communicating the same message
- personal space that is neutral or expanding without invading the personal space of others

Assertive behavior can be appropriate for many situations. It can be useful whenever we feel pressured by someone, not listened to, sucked in to another person's purpose, or uncomfortable in any way. It can create clear communication which helps build stronger relationships. Assertive behavior establishes an environment of honesty. Relationships, including those with children, built around honesty (where a person's word is always respected and we always say what we mean) can build a tradition where myths about women and children not telling the truth can be broken.

Appropriate responses for specific circumstances may be assertive, passive, or aggressive. Passive or aggressive behavior will escalate some situations. Assertive behavior, in most cases, will neutralize an exchange while communicating clearly. Comparing these behaviors helps us choose which type of behavior we want to use, rather than responding out of panic or habit. Having a choice allows us to take more control of our situations and relationships.

Learning Assertiveness Skills

Communicating assertively is more difficult and unfamiliar to many women than passive or aggressive behavior. For women who are raised to be passive and think of others before themselves, access to learning assertiveness skills is limited and using assertive behavior is a special challenge. Learning to be assertive takes time and practice. Tips for appearing assertive will be presented in the following pages.

One way to begin is to observe others. Notice how people communicate and the reactions they get. Analyze their behavior by comparing it to the lists which characterize passive, aggressive, and assertive behavior. Make notes about specific behaviors that get the reactions you like. Identify one or more people to be your assertiveness role models and pay special attention to their communication skills.

Practice being assertive in easy situations. Pick an encounter with a stranger, co-worker, friend, or family member where there is a good chance of being successful. The issue should not be very critical or be one where you might feel vulnerable or easily threatened. It can be face-to-face, over the phone, one-on-one, or with a support person.

Decide what you want to accomplish, choose the words you will say, and rehearse. During the verbal exchange use the checklist for confident body posture. State a need or opinion in a clear, straightforward manner. Try acting like or being your role model. Afterwards, analyze what happened, give yourself credit for every little thing that went well, decide on improvements, and try it again. When assertive behavior in similar encounters begins to feel comfortable, try ones that are more difficult.

The following are some basics for being assertive in situations that might become or are dangerous:

- State the obvious. For example, assertively stating "I don't want to be touched," may seem obvious and unnecessary after having repeatedly taken his hand off your body, but it needs to be assertively stated.

- Appear confident and decisive.

- It is necessary to think of one's self, not only the well-being of others.

- The facts sometimes need to be ignored in order to assert one's needs, rights, and desires. For example, you invited the assailant into your home for coffee; he is now attempting to control you. Your invitation and offer of coffee does not mean that you cannot assert your need for him to leave without his coffee when you feel threatened by him. The fact that the assailant was invited into your home and offered coffee can be ignored, assertive strategies implemented, and other defense options used.

- Past agreements or decisions do not need to be honored if they jeopardize safety.

- Use the assailant's weaknesses to one's advantage in ways that will make him listen or react appropriately. Use the list of "Other Verbal Responses" that appears later in this chapter for ideas. Intuition can help sense weaknesses and choose responses that will make him react in the manner desired.

- Know yourself. We respond positively or negatively to different types of behaviors, statements, and actions. Plan for ways to handle responses and behaviors that you know will make you feel angry or out of control.

The Broken Record

This basic, but effective, technique is characterized by the repetition of a short statement that clearly expresses a need or opinion. It is useful for avoiding being drawn into another person's purposes. The broken record technique can communicate friendliness, coldness, determination, boredom, anger, or authority depending on the voice and body language used.

In easy situations, there may be no need for repetition. In highly manipulative or threatening circumstances, many repetitions may be needed to get the desired result. To use the Broken Record:

- Project confidence by using the checklist for confident body posture presented earlier in this chapter.

- Think of a short, clear statement that expresses your feelings or needs. For example:

  - I'd like to help you but I'm unable to.
  - I don't want to talk right now.
  - Your behavior is inappropriate.
  - Leave at once.

- Sound calm by keeping the voice low but loud enough to be heard clearly. Emphasis on different words can be varied to get the desired response. Speak slowly and evenly and keep breathing.

- Repeat the statement at every opportunity. Except for a quick acknowledgment or summary of what the other person said, do not deviate from the statement. Interrupting is permitted. In threatening or abusive encounters, this technique can be used effectively by interrupting often, using a loud voice, using strong gestures, repeating the statement without waiting for responses, and not deviating from the statement at all.

Even though many women have been taught otherwise, questions posed to us do not have to be answered, especially when we feel harassed, abused, or threatened. Comments made to elicit a response can be ignored. We are not obligated to engage in conversation unless we so choose. Comments and questions that show an insensitivity or disregard for the needs or opinions we communicate are commonly used to distract, sidetrack, or manipulate us into following the wishes of others. When this is not desired, the Broken Record technique is good for keeping the situation focussed on our needs and opinions.

Practice the Broken Record technique in a role play with a supportive friend. Decide on a situation and the short statement that will be repeated. Pick roles. The person practicing the Broken Record keeps repeating the statement, interrupts, does not wait for responses to the statement, and tries different tones of voice, gestures, and body language. The other person, the aggressor, tries to distract, side track, blame, joke, deny, be negative, debate, use guilt, plead, name-call, and converse with the other person. This aggressor should make at least five to ten comments, many more than one would think necessary. Trade roles and repeat.

Try encounters involving both acquaintances and strangers. The aggressor's responses can range from non-threatening to abusive. They can be based on real or fictitious circumstances. The Appendix has ideas for situations to try.

When the Broken Record technique is used without deviating from the assigned statement, it can feel uncomfortable and rude as well as empowering and in control. Many women feel strong urges to answer the aggressor's questions, wait for the aggressor to stop talking, or deviate from the statement. Realistically, the strict Broken Record is primarily used in the most threatening situations, not often in daily interactions. Role playing the Broken Record in its most rigid form with no deviation from the repeated statement is a good way to break old patterns and learn a new verbal response. This helps build a longer continuum of responses from which to choose.

Within the continuum can be assertive responses that do not follow the strict Broken Record format. These responses can be useful in less threatening situations and be more complementary to our individual styles and personalities. They may include some of the ideas presented in "Other Verbal Responses" below.

Playing the harassing or aggressor role in Broken Record practice can be difficult, but insightful. After playing the aggressor, many women say they would stop approaching the woman responding with the Broken Record after the first or second comment. To continue harassing is difficult. They stop listening to the woman and must think only of their own goals. In other words, they have to be rude and disregard the woman's feelings in order to be so persistent. Many women think back to the times they tried being assertive in similar situations but worried about hurting the harasser's feelings. After playing the harasser role, many feel justified in using the Broken Record or any other assertive strategy.

Other Verbal Responses

The Broken Record is a good example and technique for providing a straightforward assertive response. Since people and situations are different, another strategy that works well is to use different kinds of responses to influence an assailant based on what might impact him most. Our intuition and observations of acquaintances most likely to harass, abuse, or assault us are good guides for helping us decide which responses will be effective. All of the following types of responses can work well depending on the people involved. A few are more aggressive than they are assertive.

- being funny
- using sarcasm
- imitating authorities
- acting crazy
- lying
- surprising the assailant with words or actions
- spewing insults
- showing sympathy
- using logic
- valuing morality
- being impersonal
- appealing to human emotions and qualities
- responding to emotions
- displaying emotions
- playing it cool
- applying peer pressure
- emphasizing consequences
- presenting facts
- uncovering the big picture
- dealing with the here and now
- suggesting the future and/or past
- emphasizing silence with long pauses between statements
- maintaining a barrage of words
- offering more than one choice

- sticking to one demand
- negotiating
- ignoring the situation by going away without a word, turning away, or pretending that nothing is happening

Some of these responses will feel more comfortable than others. By practicing some of the less comfortable responses in easy situations, we can expand our verbal repertoire. This will increase the number of options to choose from and prepare us for more types of situations.

The actual words we speak are only a small part of what we communicate. Practicing how we say our words, hold our bodies, express our meaning through our faces, and control our personal space can help us control the entire message we communicate to others. It is an important way to avoid and deter assault while improving our self respect and our relationships with others. As one woman said after a self-defense class, "Learning assertiveness is something that will change my life."

6

ESCAPE:
FIGHTING AND MORE

An assault has escalated to a point where the woman decides that she must escape immediately. Flying fists and feet, physical strength, and athleticism are images that are strongly associated with escape. They are considered by most people as the primary aspects of self-defense. In reality, most women escape their assailants without eliciting these images by using a variety of tactics. Some women do not even strike their assailants. Numerous tactics, including physical fighting skills, can be readily accessible and useful for women.

Contrary to popular belief, women often escape assaults successfully, including assaults that are very dangerous, as described in Chapter 2. An important factor in successful escape is a strong determination to not be assaulted. Studies show that women primarily concerned with escaping are more likely to resist successfully than those who are more worried about physical injury or death.[66]

Rarely does a woman need to incapacitate an assailant completely to escape.[67] Instead, her escape usually involves a strategy that surprises or temporarily catches an assailant off guard, giving the woman a chance to get away. Many women are able to escape, even at this stage of an assault, by convincing the assailant to stop his violence. Mean intent, described below, and verbal strategies convince many assailants to flee because they realize that controlling and dominating the situation will be difficult.

Prevention, avoidance, and/or deterrence strategies discussed in previous chapters often eliminate the need to escape. When women learn to act as soon as their intuition conveys danger, most can leave the situation before it escalates to one involving physical violence. Women prepared with escape skills, especially fighting, often feel an extra boost of confidence. This gives avoidance and deterrence strategies even greater chances for success. Basic fighting, verbal, and other strategies that have been successful for women will be described in this chapter.

Communicating Your Intention

An important part of escape is using the entire body to communicate the intention of the tactic. This means using all our effort to express that intention with our voice, facial expression, stance, words, and motions.

Many tactics such as strong verbal messages like *Go Away Now!* and fighting skills are improved with a display of mean intent. Lower the voice, make it strong and steady, scowl with the eyes and mouth, expand personal space, gesture expansively, and do everything possible with the body to present a "fierce attack tiger" image. Exaggerating all these features makes it more effective. Women who have difficulty tapping into anger or meanness can think of it as acting.

Mean intent combined with yelling has stopped many would-be assailants in their tracks.

Practice in front of a mirror. Try different mean looks. Yell, repeat a broken record statement, practice fighting skills, and try other tactics you want to use when in danger while maintaining your mean intent. Remember that people will react to your outside image (the one in the mirror), not to how you feel inside.

Fighting Back with Words

Researchers find that verbal assertiveness is among the most successful strategies used to escape assault.[68] Together with mean intent, an assertive woman communicates a strong willingness to do whatever is necessary to escape and be safe. The assailant sees that this person will not be easy to overpower and that he must contend with the outside intervention that might result. In many instances, the assailant stops the assault. The following are examples of what some women did.

- Coming out of the bathroom, a woman at a party was greeted by her friend's naked brother. He told her she wasn't leaving until they had sex. She yelled and ran out of the house.

- Two men grabbed a woman's arms and tried to drag her across a park. The men left her alone after she kept up a loud barrage of words.

- A woman woke to the noises of an intruder downstairs. She strode to the top of the stairs and bellowed, "Get out of my house now." He did.

- When a woman's husband was out of town one of his friends attempted to rape her. She yelled and protested loudly during the assault. Hearing the commotion, her landlord came to investigate. The man immediately stopped the assault and left.

- A woman's attempts at fighting off her assailant were not working. She believed that her survival was at stake when he began hitting her head with the butt of his gun. She let out several blood curdling yells. The assailant was in such a hurry to leave, he nearly tore the doors off their hinges.

Yelling

Exploding with a sound, word, or short phrase is a verbal tactic so powerful it deserves its own section. In contrast to screaming which suggests fear, yelling:

- displays confidence
- helps keep the mind and body active when fear and panic begin to set in

- surprises assailants, especially when used at close range, because women are not expected to yell
- draws attention to the situation, including the possibility of help
- increases the power of fighting skills much like a grunt helps a person lift heavy objects
- diminishes pain when released upon impact during a fall or a strike upon one's own body.

Although it can be extremely difficult for some women, many find yelling exhilarating and invigorating. Women who find yelling difficult might try relating it to calling for children or pets when they stray too far or into danger.

A yell begins with a breath that sinks down to the bottom of the lungs. It helps to think of the air being sucked or circulating deep into the abdomen. Since many people breathe only at chest level, the first step to learning to yell is to practice deep breathing.

Inhale through the nose, letting the air travel down the body, expanding the entire abdominal area. Avoid letting the chest rise. Breathe out by contracting the abdomen, squeezing the air back up and out the mouth. Rest the hands on the abdomen at or below the belly button to check that it is expanding and contracting properly with each breath. Practice this often. This practice of slow and deep breathing can also be used as a method for relaxing.

When yelling, the breaths are quick and sharp. Inhale air down to the abdomen, then expel the air quickly. A strong yell will escape when words or sounds are added. Open the mouth wide and add mean intent to become a formidable looking opponent.

Some people feel comfortable yelling words like "NO!" or "STOP!" Others yell sounds like "HAE!" or "DA!" Short phrases like "GO AWAY!" or "LEAVE ME ALONE!" help improve breath control. Women who are deaf and others who have their own kind of vocalization can yell their own unique sounds. The actual word doesn't really matter because it is the yell's loudness, suddenness, and intent that makes it effective.

There should be no pain in the throat when yelling although it is common to feel some pain when first practicing it. To relieve the pain, try lowering the voice and opening the mouth and throat wider. A word or sound ending in a vowel can help by keeping the mouth and throat open.

Many women feel uncomfortable practicing their yells because of the attention it can draw. Good ways to practice are in the shower, in the car on the freeway, or into a pillow. In situations when we need to call our children or our pets, use the principles described above. Not only will these calls most likely be louder with less stress on the throat, we will be practicing yells that can also be used when safety is threatened.

The Creative Strategy of Pretending

A creative escape strategy is to be outrageous, act in a manner that makes the situation different than it seems, or play the role of someone other than yourself. It may be easier to play roles with a stranger but many of the following examples can work with assailants who are known to the defender. This strategy can be very effective but for many women, it means letting go of worrying about what other people think or possibly being embarrassed. The following options and examples may not be useful or appropriate for all women in all situations, but each has worked well for someone at some time.

- Pretend to be pregnant or menstruating.
- Be a person with an infectious disease.
- Convince the assailant that you have a heart condition or asthma that can become a crisis if you become excited or stressed.
- Vomit, urinate, or defecate on or close to the assailant.
- Pretend to have a seizure by blinking quickly, salivating, and jerking the body.

- Laugh hysterically. When a woman's date dropped his pants for sex she did not want, she escaped by making fun of his genitals.

- One woman stopped an attack in part by convincing the assailant that she was a karate expert.

- A woman walking alone late at night was approached by a man. "Isn't the sun gorgeous!" she exclaimed. He left her alone.

- A man knocked on the door of a woman who lived in an isolated area. He said that he needed to make a phone call because his car was in a ditch. When she opened the door, he entered and threatened her loudly. She said softly, "Shshsh... You'll wake the baby," while leading him toward the door and repeating the statement. He stepped outside, she shut the door, locked it, and called the police. She had no baby.

- A woman was driving her ex-husband home when he threatened to rape her. She decided to pretend to go along with him and said, "Let's loosen up a bit and go to that great bar just down the road." He agreed. When she got to the bar, she ran inside, told the bartender to call the police, and was sheltered by the people there.

- In Stopping Rape, Pauline Bart and Patricia O'Brien write about a woman who was attacked by an assailant with a knife. She persuaded him to put the knife in a different room because it made her nervous. He also let her go to the bathroom. She convinced him to let her smoke some hash and get a beer to relax. She didn't really smoke hash or drink beer. Instead, she negotiated and used delaying tactics until she was able to grab the knife. Using her assailant's weapon against him, she forced him, half naked, to flee.[69]

Involving Others

Intervention by outsiders increases the possibility of an assailant getting caught, which is one of his biggest fears. The strategy of involving or pretending to involve others deserves more

attention than it usually receives. In instances of rape, it has been found that in almost all cases where outside intervention or the threat of outside intervention occurred, the woman was able to escape the rape attempt.[70]
Many assailants have fled when a person they weren't expecting knocked on the door.

One woman was being brutally beaten in her home. She was fighting back courageously but was unable to escape or get the assailant to leave until a friend dropped by. He fled immediately.

Although some situations, like the one above, involve the chance appearance of others, we can take control of a situation by making the assailant think that help is coming. Knowing that the presence of others is a major deterrent for assailants can be an important factor in how we design our escape strategies. While the media has featured accounts of outsiders who do nothing while a woman is raped, many women are able to use the people around them in ways that help them escape. The following are strategies which are often successful in involving others or threatening outside intervention:

- Engage the help of an individual with specific instructions. For example, point to a person and yell, "You in the blue coat, call the police." It is difficult to refuse to help when personally called upon by someone in distress. This has proved to be much more successful than yelling, "Please! Help me!"

- Pretend that a stranger is an acquaintance. A woman walking down a city street was approached by a man who had raped her in the past. She quickly crossed the street and said to a stranger, "John! I'm so glad to see you, it's been so long!" Under her breath, she asked him to go along with her and keep up the conversation. She saw the rapist watch her as he walked by. After he turned the corner, she explained the situation to the stranger, thanked him, and safely reached her destination.

- As events change, use them to make the assailant fear outside intervention. One woman saw a dog walk by while being assaulted in a park. She told the assailant that he better stop because that dog's owner may be near. She had never seen the dog before and did not know if anyone was nearby. The possibility, however, made the assailant hesitate, giving her the opportunity to run and escape safely.

- Yell for someone in the house or neighborhood even if you know the person is not there. Call to a dog (even if you don't have one) and give the command to attack. One woman escaped a gang of men who surrounded her by yelling women's names, as if she was summoning these women for help.

- Make the assailant think help is coming even if you know it isn't. If the assailant lives in your home and you both know that no one can hear your yells, a story can still be created to put doubt in his mind. Here are some examples:

  · You're expecting a friend over or a package delivered any minute. The friend can be a karate expert. The deliverer can be someone who you know looks like a super heavyweight fighter because this person regularly delivers your packages.

  · Just before the assailant arrived or while he was in the bathroom, you gave some people permission to look for their lost dog on your property or you saw someone enter the woods who will hear your yells.

  · Loudly proclaim that the neighbors are very nosy and always home. Tell the assailant that the walls are thin in your house or apartment and the neighbors always call the police when things get loud.

The assailant may not believe the story but if he hesitates, an opportunity has opened for another tactic, like running or physically fighting back, in order to escape.

Women with small children often feel vulnerable to assault. Except in cases of domestic violence, assailants often view children as outsiders who can foil their assault plans. Children who attract help by yelling, making other kinds of loud noises, and running or using the phone to call friends, neighbors, or police become helpful partners in our escape strategies.

Using Fists and Feet

Since most women don't grow up learning how to fight effectively, simple common-sense fighting principles can be very helpful. People often advise women not to fight because men are bigger and stronger than women. The most effective fighting skills (and the easiest to learn), however, do not require strength or athletic ability.

There are many benefits to learning the following fundamental principles of basic fighting skills. Women with differing physical abilities discover that their bodies can be powerful and they can fight effectively, even against a formidable opponent. In addition, learning simple fighting skills can increase a woman's confidence and self-esteem which are primary deterrents to assault.

Each person must decide when, if ever, they will use their fighting knowledge. The skills can seem violent and repulsive. It may be especially difficult to think of using these skills against family members or acquaintances, who are more likely to be assailants than strangers. Learning the basic principles of fighting, practicing basic fighting skills, and deciding in advance when these skills might be used are important aspects of safety planning.

Targets

All men, no matter what their size or strength, have places on their bodies which cannot be strengthened or protected by muscle. These places are the best targets for strikes. The targets recommended are ones which require little practice or instruction to strike effectively. Hitting them causes involuntary responses that can severely limit a person's abilities. The five primary targets are:

- Eyes. Striking one eye makes both eyes water. This temporarily blinds the person who is hit so that the other person can get away or make the next move. People often feel immobilized and freaked out when they can't see.

- Nose. The eyes automatically water when the nose is hit, causing temporary blindness.

- Throat. Pressing, even lightly, the front of the throat, the hard part or "Adam's apple", can cause a suffocating sensation. When struck, a person usually worries about breathing rather than being aggressive.

- Groin (testicles, not penis). Strikes aimed upward between the legs usually cause men to double over with all their muscles contracting. They commonly fall to the floor, curl into a ball, and vomit. One misconception about the groin is that striking it makes men angrier and more aggressive. Men may become angrier when *threatened* with strikes to the groin but strikes that meet the mark will usually, as with other targets, incapacitate them temporarily. Another commonly held belief is that the groin is hard to strike effectively because men protect it. However, men will try to protect any vulnerable area they think may be targeted. While trying to protect any one or even two target areas, a third target may be open for a strike. Tight pants (even cups) offer little protection from the well aimed, powerful kick most women are capable of delivering.

- Knees. It doesn't take much pressure to break, dislocate, or severely sprain a knee when it is struck from the front or sides. Hit from the back, however, the knee buckles and is directed into the ground causing pain but not necessarily breakage or dislocation.

Many people have heard of other target areas like the solar plexus, instep or top of the foot, shin, ears, temples, jaw, pressure points, etc. These target areas are not recommended because many are difficult to strike effectively without instruction and practice. Some of these target areas are small, surrounded by muscle, or difficult to identify. Others primarily cause pain which may not be effective on people who can ignore physical pain or can not feel it due to alcohol, drugs, or adrenalin.

(left) Following assertive attempts to get this man to leave, this woman decided to strike his eyes, a good target for a fist that is swung horizontally. Hitting one eye will make both eyes water. Leaning on the counter is a way to improve balance.

(left) A woman can effectively strike her assailant's throat with a fist that travels horizontally, even when the assailant is in front of her. Her strike is aimed at the front of his throat, at the assailant's Adam's apple, not other areas of his neck which can be protected by muscle. Her wrist is flat, making a straight line from the top of her knuckles to her elbow.

(left) A stomp to the front or either side of the knee can easily break or dislocate it. The assailant then has no way to support his weight on that leg for fighting or chasing. Many people have weak knees anyway, making this an even more vulnerable target area.

(below) The top of the fist (or the back of the hand) makes a solid weapon that can strike in many directions. This woman uses the top of her fist to strike her assailant's nose. In addition to making the eyes water, the nose bleeds easily when hit which frightens many people.

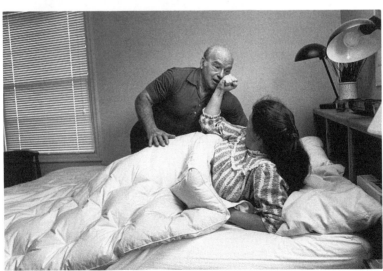

A woman whose arms are pinned in a hug from behind has many fighting options available. She can throw her head back to hit her assailant's nose, use either foot to strike his knees, or move her hips to one side like the woman in this picture to strike his groin with a fist, forearm, or "Grab, Twist, and Pull."

Strong Points — Protective Tools

Most women have strong places on their bodies that can strike these targets effectively. By using natural motions and aiming for the five primary targets, these strong places turn into protective tools which are useful and convenient. These naturally strong and powerful places are our:

- Fists, hands, and forearms. When a fist is made and squeezed tightly (thumb on the outside, across the first two knuckles), the entire lower arm becomes an effective club. There are many hitting surfaces. Open hands can be used to poke, strike, or grab targets. Fists and open hands can be used to strike at many different angles and directions. Practice by striking pillows or mattresses. It is recommended that women avoid "punching" in a forward or hooking motion with the palm down like boxers, martial artists, or police on cop shows without proper instruction.

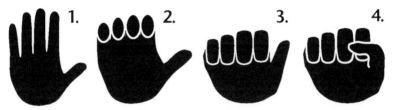

To make a fist, fold down the fingers twice, put the thumb across the outside of the first two fingers, and squeeze.

The chin can block some strikes to the throat. An open hand with fingers squeezed tightly together, thumbs pulled back, and the hand in a straight line with the arm can easily slip into the space between the chin and the collarbone for a strong strike to the front of the throat.

(left) The thumbs naturally find their targets when the other four fingers are locked behind the assailant's ears. A knee to the groin can be an effective follow-up strike if the woman decides that she needs to continue fighting.

(below) A fist that strikes too far can still be effective when the forearm hits. This assailant moved toward the woman just as she began her strike, making her fist miss his nose. Hitting the nose with her forearm, however, works just as well.

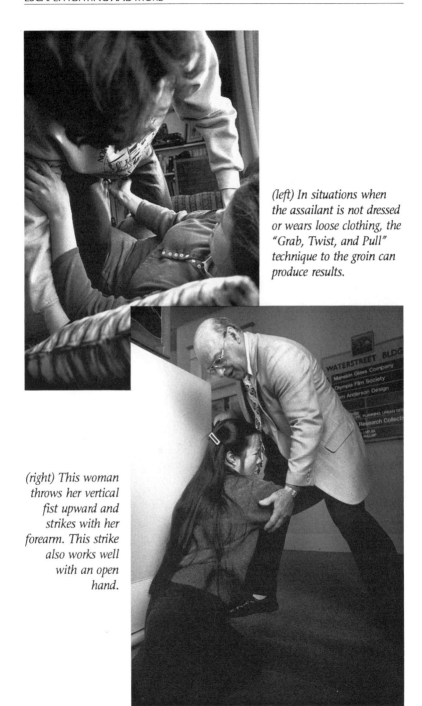

(left) In situations when the assailant is not dressed or wears loose clothing, the "Grab, Twist, and Pull" technique to the groin can produce results.

(right) This woman throws her vertical fist upward and strikes with her forearm. This strike also works well with an open hand.

- Elbows. The areas below and above the elbow effectively strike short distances. These strikes are useful against assailants who are holding you closely. Elbows can be used to strike many different angles and directions.

- Knees. A quick lift of the knee is another effective short-range strike. Feel its power by hitting your palms with a knee, one palm on top of the other and held in front of you at groin level.

Strikes with the elbow are powerful when the assailant is very close. This strike, made with the area above the elbow, is swung horizontally to slip under the assailant's jaw and into his throat. The woman may decide to follow-up with strikes to the eyes or nose.

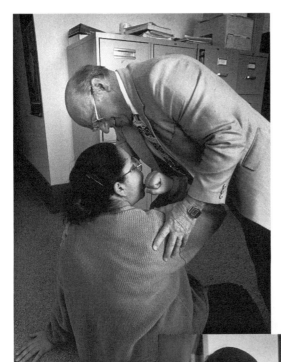

(left) In a physical confrontation, both the assailant and the woman will be in motion. Because this woman was pushed to the floor, she found an opportunity to thrust her elbow upward into her assailant's groin.

(right) While rising from her previous strike, this woman decides to knee her assailant's nose as he doubles over from her strike to his groin. Her hands on his head offers balance and helps drive his nose into her knee.

- Feet and shins. The heel of the foot can be used to stomp on an attacker's knee. The foot can be vertical or angled out in either direction. The shin and the top of the foot, where laces are on shoes, make good striking areas for kicks to the groin. Women's stomps and kicks can be very powerful because our body structure makes our hips and legs naturally stronger than our upper bodies.

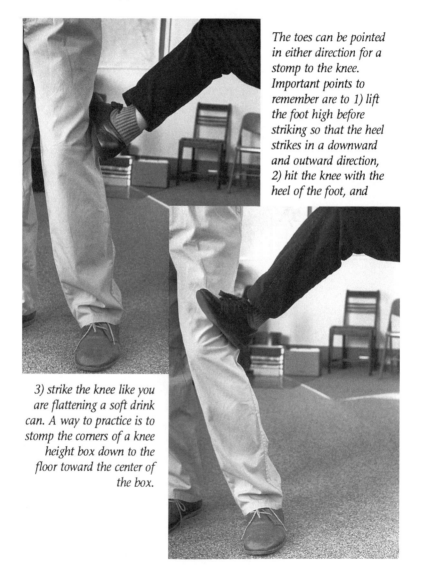

The toes can be pointed in either direction for a stomp to the knee. Important points to remember are to 1) lift the foot high before striking so that the heel strikes in a downward and outward direction, 2) hit the knee with the heel of the foot, and

3) strike the knee like you are flattening a soft drink can. A way to practice is to stomp the corners of a knee height box down to the floor toward the center of the box.

Groin kicks like this are very powerful. The hitting surface is the top of the foot or shin and the strike is upward. Lift and bend the kicking leg to start the kick, straighten the leg and point the toes when hitting the target. Use chairs, tables, walls, or attackers for balance if necessary. Notice that the distance between the woman and her assailant is greater than for the groin strike with the knee.

Strategy

Using our strong places against the attacker's target areas is the basic principle that makes it possible for people who are smaller to fight larger, stronger assailants successfully. The element of surprise is very useful for women because men usually don't expect women to fight back. When a woman does fight back, the surprise can cause an assailant to hesitate long enough for the woman to strike again, use another tactic like a verbal strategy, or get away.

In any position, whether you are sitting, pinned on the ground, held against a wall, grabbed, or choked, look for target areas that are accessible for striking. For balance grab the assailant or use a nearby chair, table, or wall. If you can't see, hold his hand, touch his arm, and feel his face to find targets. This touching can be done under the guise of caressing or "controlled" flailing. You gain information about your assailant while he thinks you are either submitting or struggling wildly.

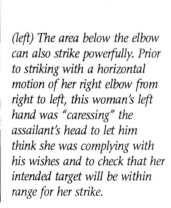

(right) While feeling her assailant's arm to confirm his position and distance, this woman strikes the assailant's nose with the heel of her palm while yelling. In a building full of people, her yell will probably attract help from others who will catch the assailant as he flees her office.

(left) The area below the elbow can also strike powerfully. Prior to striking with a horizontal motion of her right elbow from right to left, this woman's left hand was "caressing" the assailant's head to let him think she was complying with his wishes and to check that her intended target will be within range for her strike.

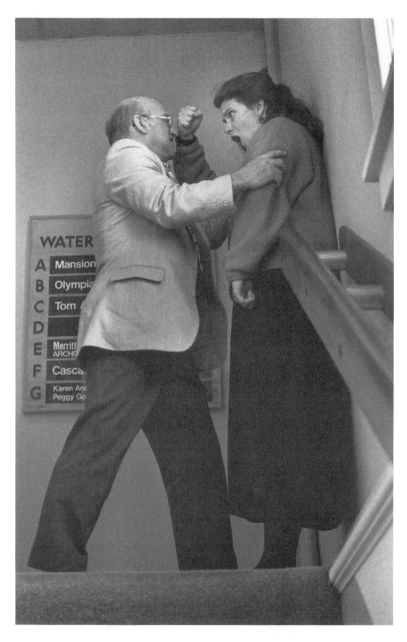

Downward hammering motions are very effective, especially to the nose.
This woman may decide to follow up her strike to the nose with kicks to the
groin or knee.

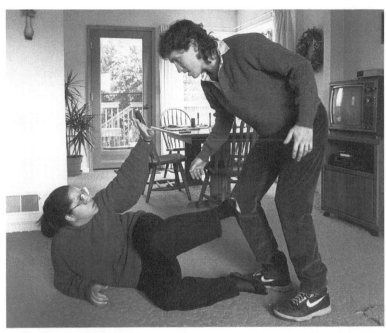

(above and right) From the ground, a woman can very effectively keep her assailant at a distance or strike targets. With an elbow, hip, and knee forming a triangle on the ground, she is in a very mobile position. She can quickly flip from her right side to her left side and back again as well as rotate her body in a circular motion pivoting on the hip. Following the attacker's knee with her foot poised to strike keeps him at bay. He risks a debilitating kick to his knee or fist to the nose when he attempts, as in these pictures, to break through her defenses.

When grabbed or held in any position, a woman usually has an arm or leg that is available to strike accessible targets on the assailant. In this example of an assailant grabbing the woman's wrist, his targets are all potentially vulnerable to strikes. The woman has one arm and both legs free. When a target is hit, he will most likely let go of her or loosen his grip. She can decide to keep striking targets, use other options like verbal strategies, or escape.

(right) In a choke hold from the front, all targets on the assailant are accessible to strikes and the woman has both arms and legs available to strike them. Any strong, well aimed strike to a target will probably cause the assailant to at least loosen his grip. Some strikes, however, can also break the assailant's grip on their way to a target. In preparation for a downward strike with the top of the fist to the assailant's nose, this woman lifts her arm high. Her entire shoulder

is lifted so that when she twists her upper body, her upper arm can cross over the top of his left forearm.

(left) The hold is broken when the elbow falls, the arm opens up, and the top of the fist strikes the nose. Being prepared to follow this strike with a knee to the groin is an option.

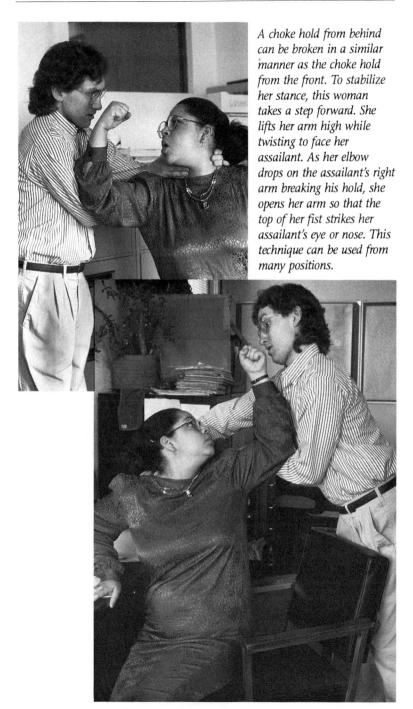

A choke hold from behind can be broken in a similar manner as the choke hold from the front. To stabilize her stance, this woman takes a step forward. She lifts her arm high while twisting to face her assailant. As her elbow drops on the assailant's right arm breaking his hold, she opens her arm so that the top of her fist strikes her assailant's eye or nose. This technique can be used from many positions.

Many people have better use of some limbs or a stronger side of the body. Strengthening and practicing with the strong parts of our bodies will improve the fighting options that use those parts of the body. For example, if making fists is difficult due to arthritis, strikes made with the forearm, open hand, knees, and feet can be practiced. When kicking is impossible due to injury, the arms and hands can often be strengthened and used for strikes. Using weapons of opportunity (described later in this chapter) can be an important strategy. Some people can increase their options by trying to strengthen and practice with the weaker parts of their bodies.

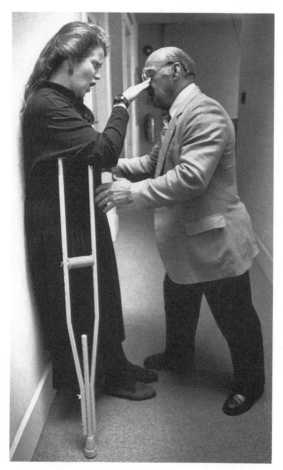

An open hand with fingers squeezed tightly together and thumb pulled back can be useful for women who have difficulty making fists. It can be substituted for most fisted strikes and is also useful for striking an eye when the assailant wears glasses. Removing those glasses can put him at a great disadvantage. Leaning against a wall can be helpful when balance is a problem.

Holding onto the attacker not only improves this woman's balance, it can also divert his attention and make him be at the perfect distance for a strong strike from the woman's knee to his groin.

Strike by using natural motions. Swinging the arms to the side is very much like opening or shutting a door. Downward strikes are like hammering or pounding on a table. Stomping on the knee is like smashing an aluminum soft drink can. Kicking the groin is like kicking a ball high and far over a tall fence.

Most women find that swinging the fist horizontally feels natural and can be very powerful. This woman is striking with the top of her fist (the back of her hand). Striking horizontally with the palm of the fist facing down, photo on page 86, also makes good use of this motion.

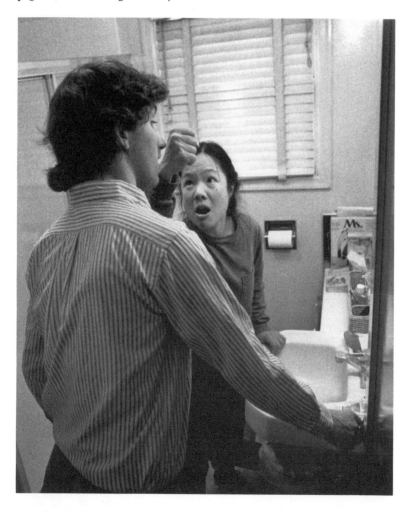

In many situations, one strike will not produce the desired results. Try striking again to the same target or another target. It is helpful to think of all fighting strategies as combinations of many strikes. Choosing to include other tactics (yelling, talking, running, involving others, playing roles, pretending to give in) can be very effective. As described in Chapter 2, studies show women having a greater chance of escaping an assault when they try many tactics.

At least one target on the assailant will be within striking distance most of the time and you will have arms or legs available to strike the target. If the assailant immobilizes your arms and legs, he is probably incapable of assaulting you further until he moves. In this situation, one strategy is to wait. When he moves to strike or remove clothing, one of your arms or legs may be freed to strike targets.

In the unlikely case that there is more than one attacker, think of the situation as an opportunity to hit more targets. Try to keep the mind active and control fear by breathing deeply and continuously, using the checklist for confident body posture, and/or yelling. There are several fighting strategies. One is to focus on the leader. If he becomes surprised, confused, or hurt, the others will often discontinue the assault. Another is to make an example out of one of the assailants by hurting him until he begs the others to call it off. Many women have escaped from multiple assailants. Some escape by being verbally assertive, striking, using any of the other tactics described, or combining a few or all of these options.

The key to effective fighting is to be completely committed to delivering each strike to its target while displaying mean intent. For more powerful strikes, breath out or yell when the strike hits its target. Strike through the target so that the strike will end several feet beyond the target, rather than at its surface. It is not uncommon for men to back off completely, even before the first strike, when confronted with a woman who verbally or non-verbally communicates her intent and commitment to strike with power at the assailant's vulnerable target areas.

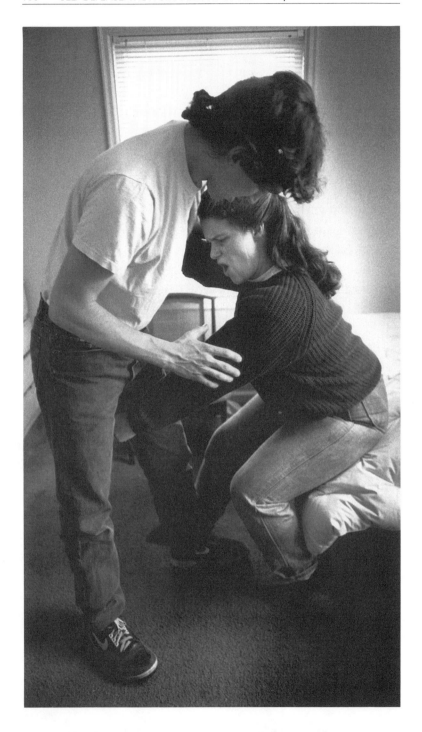

(above) The woman is close enough to her assailant that when she extends her leg, she will strike through his knee rather than stopping it at its surface. Striking through the target with proper distance, visualization, and intent is important for powerful strikes.

(opposite) Throwing a vertical fist upward into an assailant's groin is very practical in some situations. Breathing out or yelling, striking through the target, and squeezing the fist tightly make all strikes more solid and powerful.

A disadvantage for many women is our doubts about being able to win in a fight. Visualizing ourselves as successful in dangerous situations is one way to look at ourselves as capable defenders of our safety. While in a safe environment, visualize a situation you might need to escape. See yourself as strong and successful while resisting with all the skills and options you choose to use in the situation. Practice the skills alone or with supportive friends. The more our bodies and minds practice what we want to do, the more chances we have that they will work when needed in a real situation.

These women are finding out that strikes with their knees and elbows can be very strong and debilitating if a target is hit. Strikes can be practiced by hitting the palms held at target level. To reduce the stinging in the palms from repeated strikes, rub them together vigorously before and after this exercise.

Weapons of Convenience

Nearby objects can be used to strike targets on assailants, block the assailant's attacks, or provide barriers between the assailant and the defender. They can be used to extend our reach. Everyday items can be turned into weapons that help us escape assault.

Hot coffee, skillets, plants, hair spray or other sprays, baseball bats, brooms, keys laced between the fingers, crutches, cane, the pet cat, spike heels on shoes, telephone receivers, pens, toothbrushes, and scrap lumber are examples of common household items that can be used to strike vital targets. A wheelchair can be used to ram the assailant, back into him, or run over his foot. Its foot rest can strike ankles or shins. A woman on her bike rammed the front wheel between her assailant's legs, striking his groin so she could get away. Another woman trapped her assailant's arm in her car's window by rolling it up when he reached inside.

This woman follows up her strike to the assailant's eye with an upward strike to his groin. If the assailant falls backward after the first strike, her crutches will extend her reach. Women with poor balance or who cannot kick can use long objects as a substitute for the groin kick.

*(above) Anything in a room, even a bathroom, can be
used to strike targets on an assailant.*

*(opposite, above) Striking with short weapons is like using a fist with added
reinforcement. For this woman, the phone receiver was already in her hand,
making it a convenient weapon.*

*(opposite, below) Long weapons, like brooms and crutches, can hit targets in
many ways. They can mimic the striking motions of arms by swinging
vertically, sweeping horizontally, or as in this picture, thrusting. Many can be
held at either end or anywhere in the middle to control length. The tips can
strike, as in this picture, or the middle can be used as a bar.*

A pan, bag of groceries, or heavy handbag can be held or swung into the path of an assailant's strike to block it from landing on one's body. A woman using a wheelchair can try turning it just before a strike lands so that the assailant strikes the chair. Couches, tables, and chairs can be used to barricade entrances or be arranged as an obstacle course to slow down the assailant.

(above) Flat weapons, like this skillet, can be used to block an incoming strike. The woman's loud yell when the assailant's strike hits will not only surprise him, it will strengthen her ability to receive the blow.

(opposite, left) The edge of a flat weapon, like this book, can be used to strike vulnerable targets. To remain stable while standing, the woman's feet are flat on the floor shoulder width apart with one foot forward and both knees slightly bent.

Some things can be used as a barrier to slow down the assailant. Being assaulted in one's own home can be an advantage because its familiarity can help with identifying escape routes and locating items that can be used as weapons of opportunity.

Should I Carry a Gun?

Carrying a weapon, such as a gun, knife, or spray device like mace, is a self-defense option which women must decide for themselves whether or not to use. The following considerations are important for successfully using weapons in self-defense:

1. A woman who uses the weapon (shoots, cuts, or sprays to do harm) as soon as she shows it during an assault will most likely defend herself successfully. A weapon used for intimidation can be taken away and used against her. Emotional and legal consequences are important considerations in the decision to carry and use a weapon.

2. If a woman decides that she can and will use the weapon when she shows it during an assault, then a commitment should be made to learn about its proper use and to practice using it regularly. Even seemingly simple weapons like spray devices take knowledge, practice, and familiarity to use effectively.

The decision to carry a gun brings unique considerations such as legal issues and safety during storage, especially in households with children. Information on gun use and storage is available through classes taught by the police as well as private organizations and individuals. Women may want to attend these in groups for mutual support.

What if the Assailant Has a Weapon?

Facing an armed assailant is a frightening experience. The fear can be compounded by an unfamiliarity with weapons and an association of weapons with death and mutilation. As the statistics regarding weapon use in Chapter 3 show, very few assailants armed with a gun or knife actually use their weapon. Serious injuries are few among those wounded and even fewer die.

One report revealed that "In 87% of the nonfatal crimes involving handguns, the offender did not fire the weapon but used it to intimidate."[71] Another found that "For guns in particular it appears that the weapon may be used by the offender to coerce the victim into meeting demands rather than to injure the victim."[72] Although these reports make no claims regarding self-defense, this fact can greatly affect the kinds of self-defense decisions a person might make when faced with a weapon. If one receives an intuitive feeling that an armed attacker is using the weapon primarily for coercion, the accuracy of that message is statistically substantiated. Decisions regarding self-defense options can be made accordingly.

Many self-defense experts, including individuals in law enforcement, agree that attackers intending to hurt their victims with their weapons usually use their weapons immediately upon showing them or initiating the assaults. An attacker who makes demands and threatens to use the weapon if his demands are not met is probably using it primarily for coercion. Whether he is psychologically capable of hurting or killing his victim is unknown. This is where intuition can play an important role in decisions regarding defensive strategies.

In assaults against women, assailants who use their weapons for coercion probably do not consider what they would do if the women resisted. They may not be prepared to shoot, cut, or kill their victims when their demands are not met. Women are not expected to fight back in any assault, let alone one where a weapon is present. The assailant is likely to be surprised when faced with a woman's resistance. This surprise can be used to the woman's advantage. She can strike targets on the assailant (while being aware of the weapon's position), attempt other defense options, or run. The choice to resist lies with the woman. It is based on her abilities and knowledge of the situation.

Resisting an armed assailant is probably one of the most feared self-defense scenarios. Decisions regarding defense strategies can be based on accurate information about the motivation behind weapon use, the fact that the chances of actually being shot or cut are slim, and the likelihood of surviving weapon wounds is good. Many women have successfully resisted armed assailants. As in situations without weapons, they used a variety of options and relied on their intuition to guide their reactions.

Successful escape involves determination, making choices, knowing our strengths, and transforming the situation to our advantage. Age, disability, or a lack of athletic prowess does not have to limit a woman's ability to escape assaults. Safety planning, quick thinking and use of intuitive clues, strong communication of intent, confidence and assertiveness, loud yells, stories, outsiders, and strategies for striking targets on the assailant are the important factors to successful escape. We can improvise ways that allow us to use our abilities to our advantage. Escape becomes possible when the assailant hesitates, stops, or leaves the situation because of surprise, pain, or a need to reconsider continuing the assault.

7

SURVIVAL

Self-defense cannot stop at escape. It must also include issues of survival: survival choices during an assault and survival after an assault. Because all assaults are traumatic experiences, surviving an assault is a great accomplishment. We need to be proud of the fact that we do the best we can, no matter what happens during the assault. An assault is not over, however, once the assailant is gone. Surviving the aftermath includes important choices that can help us feel safe again. We can also use this information to help other women survive and recover emotionally from their assaults. These aspects of survival will be covered in this chapter.

Survival Choices During Assault

Women always do the best they can during an assault. Defense plans may seem, at times, to disappear in moments of fear and panic. Under these circumstances, many women surprise them-selves by instinctive actions that seem to take over while others may feel that there is nothing they can do to resist the assailant.

In some situations, women sometimes find that complying with the assailant's demands is a choice that feels necessary in order to survive. For whatever reason, submitting in an assault is a valid self-defense option for women to choose. It does not imply that she is consenting to violence.

Women who survive such situations develop strategies to help protect themselves emotionally, both during and after the assault. These tactics help keep their sense of self-worth and dignity intact. The following are some of the many strategies that can help women not only endure an assault, but also recover faster after the assault. Some can turn into escape tactics:

- Deciding to "give in" can be thought of, instead, as "waiting". As the situation changes, more defense options may become available and new choices made. It is not unusual for an assailant to loosen his guard when he thinks the woman has "given in".

- One woman decided to focus her mind on prosecuting her assailant. She memorized every detail about the assault and her assailant with the intention of using this information to build her case in court. This also kept her mind active while "waiting" so she could be ready if new defense options appeared.

- Repeat to yourself or aloud, "This is not my fault. I am doing the best I can. I am a good person. I will survive."

- A way to mentally focus on survival is to visualize the people you love, the important things you do, or other elements of your "survival image", a mental picture that gives you strength (see Chapter 1). During an assault, draw on the image for energy, courage, and the motivation to persist and endure.

- All of us have a place inside that no other person can touch, invade, degrade, or destroy. In this place is who we are, our individuality, and our self-worth. Because we have total control of this place, assailants can never overpower us completely. Focusing on this place during an assault can give us the confidence and strength to survive.

Self-defense has now formed a complete circle by coming back to the importance of nurturing ourselves. Caring about ourselves not only motivates us to take action to protect our safety as described in Chapter 1, it also is a primary element of survival. Finding time in our daily lives to focus on our needs, finding out what we like about ourselves, and doing things that fulfill us will improve the quality of our lives in general. It will make the survival image strong inside us. Being aware of the special place in ourselves that is all ours and doing things to nurture it will help the place grow. Visualizing your survival image often and nurturing the special place regularly can make them more accessible during an assault. In times of danger, caring about ourselves helps us survive.

After the Assault: Surviving the Opinions of Others

Going on with our lives after an assault can be a special challenge. Myths we live with about assault can haunt us and break down our knowledge that we did the best we could and that the assault was not our fault. Other people, including those we might go to for support, also live with these myths. Increased public education about assault against women has resulted in much improvement in the support available to assault survivors. However, it is difficult for people to change the attitudes they grew up with and internalized, even people with the best intentions. When approaching people for help, we may not find the support we need.

It is common for women to relive the situation in order to analyze what happened and try to make some sense of it. Myths in our society try to make everyone, including ourselves, believe that the woman must have done something to cause the assault. We commonly berate ourselves with thoughts such as:

- I should have known better and not...
- He must have misunderstood me. I should have been more assertive.
- I didn't want to hurt his feelings and so I let him take advantage of me.
- If I make myself more unappealing, maybe men would stop thinking of me that way.
- I must have done something to make him think he could...

People often try to analyze the assaults of others in similar ways. Rather than placing the blame for the assault squarely on the assailant, these sentiments all point to the woman being responsible for the man's violence in some way. We must destroy the myth that women are to blame for the violence they experience by reminding ourselves that the assault is never our fault. It is important to find support from people who share this understanding.

Everyone, including ourselves, wants to look for ways to respond better in the situation. People often say, "That was a stupid thing to do," or "You should have done this," or "When I was attacked, I..." Our responses may include, "I wish I had done...," "I could have gotten away sooner, if only I had done...," or "I can't believe that I didn't think of doing..." However, the assault is over and the outcome will not be different. We did the best we could in the situation and no one else can ever do better because they were not in it with us.

Women often report a lack of understanding shown toward assault survivors among law enforcement, medical, and legal professionals. Attitudes that blame the woman for the assault and judge her defensive tactics still persist even though more support-ive individuals now work in these fields. The decision to report an assault to authorities is a personal one that can be made at any time after the assault. If the intent of reporting is to prosecute the assailant, however, immediate reporting (even before showering) is necessary. Being accompanied by a support person, whether that person is a friend, family member, or worker from a sexual or domestic violence crisis center, can be extremely helpful.

Finding emotional support after an assault is very important. Because we are all different, the support we need will be different for each of us. Some women will prefer to be with friends and others will find supportive family members. Many agencies which support victims of sexual assault and domestic violence have hotlines where people can receive anonymous support. Some of these agencies also provide information, counseling, shelter, and other services. The Appendix has information on these agencies. Counselors trained to assist women who survive assault can help women sort out their feelings and regain a sense of control in their lives. Others in helping professions such as medical workers, clergy, and teachers, can also provide excellent support.

Since concern about assaults experienced by women is grow-ing, options for finding support are increasing. Intuition plays a large part in choosing the type of support that will best suit each individual. If getting help from one person does not feel right, try someone else. Sometimes another person in the same agency might be the perfect one. After having survived an assault, finding help that meets our needs can seem formidable. Even though it may require several tries, good support is worth the effort.

Helping a Survivor After Her Assault

A woman has experienced an assault and is reaching out for support. She can be anyone. Her descriptions and reactions can make us feel overwhelmed. All kinds of emotions may come up, including ones that surface when memories of assaults we experienced are triggered. We may feel intimidated by the responsibility of the situation. The following are some guidelines to prepare ourselves for supporting others who have been assaulted.

- Make this time just for her. Listen without judgment, personal opinions, advice, or personal stories. Let her talk at her own speed. Find out what she needs and respond positively to her requests. Comfort her with whatever helps her feel secure and loved. Get help for your own needs and emotions from someone else at another time.

- Believe her. Since most of the violence women experience does not resemble the conventional concept of assault, a woman's greatest fear might be not being believed or having her experience minimized as "not that bad." Encourage her to express her feelings freely and validate those feelings.

- Guarantee confidentiality. Regaining a sense of control in her life can be an assault survivor's largest hurdle. Letting her choose who knows about her experience is a tangible way for her to regain some control. Confidentiality can also be important for her safety.

- Inform the woman of assault facts. Reassuring information includes an understanding that assault is common, all women are at risk of assault, she is not alone in her feelings, the assault was not her fault, and she did the best she could in the situation.

- Present options, respect her choices, and respond to her wishes. These are ways to help the woman retrieve a sense of control over her life.

- Help the woman with safety issues. Suggest options and support her choices. If she asks about preventing future assault, talk about trusting her intuition, acting quickly, using as many defense options as possible, and trying many defense strategies. Make a safety plan (see Appendix). Assure her that whatever she does is the best she can do at that time. There are no right or wrong options.

- Assure the woman that continuing help and support is available. If you are unable to provide that help, be sure to set your own limits and communicate them clearly. Suggest referrals to other people or agencies.

Women are survivors. Through pain, abuse, harassment, and assault, whether it is physical or emotional, women of all ages, abilities, and cultures survive and endure. By creating our own definition for success and survival rather than using the definitions handed to us by our male dominated society, we open ourselves up to a treasure chest of strategies that women have used successfully to protect their safety. We learn the art of being safe by listening to the stories of other women and sharing our own experiences.

From prevention to survival, we find that self-defense is making choices. The effort to make these choices is motivated by the desire to protect ourselves, a desire kindled by the sense of self we have nurtured. The choices we eventually make are guided by our intuition. Self-care, intuition, and choice: qualities that can save us from abuse and assault, qualities that can inspire us to be the women we want to be.

ENDNOTES

1   Many of the women who experienced these successes were students in FIST's self-defense classes. They shared these stories as examples of how women naturally defend themselves when faced with danger. Other stories were reported in local newspapers.

2   Pauline B. Bart, "Avoiding Rape: A Study of Victims and Avoiders," Final Report, NIMH, 1980.

     Vernon L. Quinsey, Douglas Upfold, "Rape Completion and Victim Injury As A Function Of Female Resistance Strategy," Canadian Journal of Behavioral Science, Vol. 17 (1), 1985, p. 40-50.

3   Pauline B. Bart, p. 18-19.

4   Robbie C. Burnett, Donald I. Templer, and Patrick C. Barker, in "Personality Variables and Circumstances of Sexual Assault Predictive of a Woman's Resistance," Archives of Sexual Behavior, Vol. 14, No. 2, 1985, p. 183-187. This study found that women who strongly resisted assault were less anxious about dying as a result of the assault, were assertive, and generally perceived themselves as being in control over their destiny.

5   Joyce Levine-MacCombie, Mary P. Koss, "Acquaintance Rape: Effective Avoidance Strategies," Psychology of Women Quarterly, Vol. 10, 1986, p. 318.

6   Pauline B. Bart, p. 24.

7   Pauline B. Bart, p. 20-22.

8   Jennie J. McIntyre, "Victim Response to Rape: Alternative Outcomes," Final Report, NIMH, 1979, Question 12, p. 6.

9   "Queens Bench Foundation Study, Part III. Conclusions," LEAA, 1976, p. 4.

10   Eugene J. Kanin, "Date Rape: Unofficial Criminals and Victims," Victimology: An International Journal, Vol. 9, 1984, p. 102.

11   Judith Siegal, Susan B. Sorenson, Jacqueline M. Golding, M. Audrey Burnam, and Judith A. Stein, "Resistance to Sexual Assault: Who Resists and What Happens?" American Journal of Public Health, Vol. 79, No. 1, January, 1989, p. 31. It is shown that women are more likely to resist and receive injuries because of the sexual assault than that the assault and the injuries being received are the result of their resistance.

12   Vernon L. Quinsey, et al, p. 48.

13   Pauline B. Bart, p. 12-14.

14   Pauline B. Bart, p. 22.

15   Mary P. Koss, Christine A. Gidycz, and Nadine Wisniewski, "The Scope of Rape: Incidence and Prevalence of Sexual Aggression and Victimization in a National Sample of Higher Education Students," Journal of Consulting and Clinical Psychology, Vol. 55, No. 2, 1987, p. 169. These researchers found that only 5% of the 886 instances of rape and attempted rape involving university students were reported to police. 5% of the women sought victim assistance services, 27% identified their experience as rape, and 42% told no one. These researchers also state that the government estimates that one rape is reported for every three to ten rapes committed.

     Mary P. Koss, "The Hidden Rape Victim: Personality, Attitudinal, and Situational Characteristics," Psychology of Women Quarterly, Vol. 9, 1985, p. 197. 48% of the women in this study who acknowledged that they had been raped did not discuss their rape with anyone. More than half of those who did not recognize their victimization as rape also told no one.

16   The following account is a summary of "The Women's Self-defense Movement: A Study of the Methods and Trends of Women's Resistance to Male Violence in America," an unpublished paper by Staci Cotler, Portland, Oregon, 1990.

17 Jerome Nadelhaft, "Wife Torture: A Known Phenomena In Nine-
    teenth Century America," Journal of American Culture, Volume
    10, 1986-1987, p. 53.

18 Christine Stansell, City of Women: Sex and Class in New York,
    1789-1860, Alfred A. Knopf, 1986, p. 81.

19 Linda Gordon, "The Politics of Child Sex Abuse," Against the
    Current, March/April, 1989, p. 40.

20 Susan Schecter, Women And Male Violence: The Visions and
    Struggles of the Battered Women's Movement, South End Press,
    1982, p. 13.

21 Mary P. Koss, et al, "The Scope of Rape...," p. 166.

    Eugene J. Kanin, "Date Rape: Unofficial Criminals and Victims,"
    Victimology: An International Journal, Vol. 9, No. 1, 1984, p. 95,
    98. In addition to finding that rapists in his study rarely encoun-
    tered the criminal justice system as a result of their assaults, had
    no history of violence, and did not display impulsive behavior,
    Kanin strongly states that studying rape by working with institu-
    tionalized rapists is "inordinately biased." It is estimated that only
    10% of rapes are reported. Two to 64% of these are considered
    "unfounded." Offenders in only half of the "founded" cases are
    apprehended. Of these, three-fourths are prosecuted but 50% are
    dismissed or acquitted. It is estimated that less than 3% of re-
    ported rapes end in rape convictions. Kanin states, "Our knowl-
    edge about the rapist, then, is essentially derived from the study of
    criminal failures, that very small percentage of offenders who are
    not only apprehended but also convicted."

    K. Daniel O'Leary, "Physical Aggression Between Spouses: A Social
    Learning Theory Perspective," Handbook of Family Violence,
    Plenum Press, 1988, p. 40.

    Carl A. Bersani and Huey-Tsyh Chen, "Sociological Perspectives in
    Family Violence," Handbook of Family Violence, Plenum Press,
    1988, p. 68.

22 Diana Russell, Sexual Exploitation: Rape, Child Sexual Abuse,
    and Workplace Harassment, Sage Library of Social Research,
    Vol. 155, 1984, p. 67. In a study based on a sample taken from the
    general population, only 0.7% of rapes involved female rapists. In
    most of these cases, the woman participated in the assault with
    one or more male rapists.

23 Diana Russell, p. 69-73.

24 Diana Russell, p. 285.

25 Ellen Ryerson, "Providing Counseling And Advocacy For Handi-
    capped Persons Who Have Been Sexually Abused: A Training
    Manual For Staff And Volunteers," Seattle Rape Relief, 1981, p. 4.

26 Robin Warshaw, I Never Called It Rape, Harper & Row, 1988,
    p. 11.

27 Eugene J. Kanin, p. 102-103.

28 Mary P. Koss, "The Hidden Rape Victim...," p. 210. Ms. Koss
    concluded that a woman who acknowledged experiencing a
    situation that fit the legal definition of rape but did not identify
    that experience as rape "appeared to encounter her sexual assault
    in the context of a close personal relationship and shared sexual
    intimacy that disqualified the experience as rape in the victim's
    mind."

29 Robin Warshaw, p. 26.

30 Jennie J. McIntyre, Question 12, p. 6.

31 Diana Russell, p. 286.

32 Peter V. DiVasto, Arthur Kaufman, Lynn Rosner, Rebecca Jackson,
    Joan Christy, Sally Pearson, Terry Burgett, "The Prevalence of
    Sexually Stressful Events Among Females in the General Popula-
    tion," Archives of Sexual Behavior, Vol. 13, No. 1, 1984, p. 63.

33 The 12/27/89 issue of The Olympian (Olympia, WA) reported that
    of the 23,899 children counted as missing since the National
    Center for Missing and Exploited Children opened in 1984, "only
    511 have been snatched by strangers."

34 K. Daniel O'Leary, "Physical Aggression Between Spouses: A Social
    Learning Theory Perspective," Handbook of Family Violence,
    Plenum Press, 1988, p. 37.

35 Evan Stark and Anne Flitcraft, "Violence Among Intimates: An
    Epidemiological Review," Handbook of Family Violence, Plenum
    Press, 1988, p. 301.

36 Federal Bureau of Investigation, 1982, and U.S. Department of
    Justice, 1985.
    More information about homicides between partners is available in
    Angela Browne's, "Family Homicide: When Victimized Women
    Kill," Handbook of Family Violence, Plenum Press, 1988, p. 275.

37 "Queen's Bench...," p. 2.
    Susan Schechter, p. 219-224.

38 Diana Russell, p. 111-168, explores several theories, documented
    with research, on the cause of rape.
    Mildred Daley Pagelow, Family Violence, Praeger Publishers, 1984,
    p. 97-105. This well-documented discussion of the "power/
    powerlessness" dynamic within family violence attempts to answer
    why some men resort to violence while others in similar circum-
    stances do not.

39 Diana Russell, p. 117-123.

40 "Queen's Bench...," p. 2.

41 Susan Schecter, p. 228-231. Information is presented on how the
    roles men play in the family and male socialization can result in
    violence.

42 Mildred Daley Pagelow, p. 117-121.

43 Eugene J. Kanin, p. 98-99.
    Mildred Daley Pagelow, p. 127-142. Additional information on the
    effect of sex role socialization, role models, the media and sports
    in promoting violence against women is presented.

44 Diana Russell, p. 47. A random sample revealed 44% of women
    have experienced rape or attempted rape. It does not include other
    types of assault.

45 Mary P. Koss, et al, "The Scope of Rape..." and Mary P. Koss "The
    Hidden Rape Victim...." See Note 15.

46 Mary P. Koss, et al, "The Hidden Rape Victim...," p. 196-197. 43%
    of the women who acknowledged experiencing a situation that fit
    the legal definition of rape did not identify that experience as rape
    in this study.

47 Mary P. Koss, et al, "The Scope of Rape...," p. 168.

48 Peter V. DiVasto, et al, p. 61.

49 Mary P. Koss, et al, "The Scope of Rape...," p. 166.

50 This data represents all sexual assaults reported to rape crisis
    centers in Massachusetts from August 1983 to April 1986 covering
    5,533 cases.

51 Eugene J. Kanin, p. 99.

52   Data from Massachusetts' rape crisis centers shows that most of the assaults that did occur outdoors were committed by strangers.

53   Jennie J. McIntyre, Question 12, p. 5.

54   "Queen's Bench...," p. 2.

55   Michael R. Rand, "Handgun Crime Victims," Bureau of Justice Statistics Special Report, July 1990. Unless otherwise noted, the statistics that follow are disclosed in this report. Its data was obtained from the National Crime Survey for 1979 to 1987. It studied a yearly average of 639,900 crimes committed with handguns out of an annual average of 6,668,000 violent crimes.

56   "The Use of Weapons in Committing Crimes," Bureau of Justice Statistics Special Report, 1986. The data represents 65 million victimizations covering ten years, 1973 to 1982. It is based on a survey of households with crimes against commercial establishments not included.

57   "The Use of Weapons in Committing Crimes."

58   "The Use of Weapons in Committing Crimes."

59   "The Use of Weapons in Committing Crimes."

60   Robin Warshaw, p. 152.

61   Intuitive hunches are verified when women learn that a person was assaulted at the time and location revealed by their intuition or a person was arrested at the same time and place for loitering or other anti-social behavior. Many of these situations involve strangers.

62   Margo Adair, Working Inside Out, Tools For Change, Wingbow Press, 1984, p. 80.

63   "Queen's Bench...," p. 2.

64   Barrie Levy, Skills for Violence-Free Relationships: Curriculum for Young People Ages 13-18, Southern California Coalition on Battered Women, Network Publications, 1984, p. 65. Several of these behaviors were presented in this publication.

65   Barrie Levy, p. 63.

66   Pauline B. Bart, p. 20-21.

67   Jennie J. McIntyre, Question 12, p. 8.

68   Vernon L. Quinsey, et al, p. 48.

69 Pauline B. Bart and Patricia H. O'Brien, <u>Stopping Rape</u>, Pergamon Press, 1985, p. 54.

70 Pauline B. Bart, p. 19.

71 Michael R. Rand, p. 1.

72 "The Use of Weapons in Committing Crimes."

APPENDIX

Helping Children Protect Themselves

The common occurrence of child abuse and child sexual assault leads to many questions about protecting children from violence and teaching children to defend themselves. It is important to remember that children are almost always assaulted or abducted by people they know. Boys are abused and assaulted as well as girls. Instead of force, bribes of presents and affection or threats to the child or others the child cares about are commonly used to coerce a child sexually.

We can use any opportunity to educate our children about the facts of assault and how to prevent them. The best information is clear, accurate, and given when kids ask for it or are able to understand it. It is common to discuss assault prevention in the framework of safety, along with crossing streets and preventing fires. Talk about sexual assault in terms of uncomfortable or bad touch, in comparison with good touch. Straightforward information that is not shrouded in fear or secrecy usually does not frighten children.

Children also learn about these issues from the attitudes of adults around them and by watching how these adults relate to each other. Adults who try to communicate clearly, be confident and assertive, and avoid abusive relationships teach children valuable lessons in self-defense daily.

Ourselves as Children

Looking at our childhoods can be revealing. We can reflect on how childhood messages about our bodies, sexual assault, and relationships to adults affect our ability to protect ourselves from abuse or assault. Some misleading messages children often receive are:

- Watch out for strangers. (Kids are almost always assaulted by family or acquaintances. This message can confuse kids who are expected to talk to some adults they are not acquainted with.)

- Don't take candy from strangers. (This statement does not tell kids why bribes are dangerous. Adults say that as children, they thought something was wrong with the candy.)

- People that hurt kids are sick. (A child may think that these people would be easy to identify because they will be in bed, throwing up, wearing bandages...)

- Boys should stick up for themselves but girls should stay at home and be protected. (This message tells girls that they are not as capable as boys and cannot or should not defend themselves. Boys may learn that they must be tough and cannot be afraid.)

- Don't go out by yourself because bad things can happen. (Kids need to know what bad things to look out for.)

- Obey your father. (Kids taught to be unconditionally obedient can feel that they must obey adults even when they abuse or assault them.)

- Kiss everyone goodnight. (Children forced to have physical contact with adults can feel that they have no control over who touches them and how.)

- The big bad monster will get you if you are bad. (Kids who are abused or assaulted may feel that they are to blame for the violence because they were bad. They may also look for a "monster" to hurt them rather than a friend or family member.)

Teaching Our Kids to Defend Themselves

The following recommendations can help kids protect themselves.

- Give children clear and accurate information about who may hurt them and how it might happen.

- Remind them that even "nice" people sometimes do mean things.

- Leave them only in the care of people who are trusted.

- Prepare them to deal with bribes, secrets, threats, and physical force.

- Let them say "No" to hugs, kisses, and other touches that feel uncomfortable to them. Respect their wishes and encourage others to do the same.
- Help them list people they can talk to when somebody makes them uncomfortable. Reassure children that those people will do whatever they can to protect them.
- Teach kids the words for talking about their bodies and let them use these words.
- Give them opportunities to make choices (clothing, food, toys...)
- Let kids see you being confident and assertive, trusting your intuition, not allowing abuse in your relationships, and choosing to only be with people you trust to not be violent or abusive.

Kids are most likely to talk to adults about these issues when adults take them seriously. Following up on information children disclose about their abuse, assault, or suspicions helps reassure them that everything possible is being done to help them.

Identifying Characteristics

Noticing details is a skill that can help us increase general awareness, identify greater numbers of defense options, and keep our minds actively focussed on the present. Detailed descriptions are often used to locate individuals and investigate assault situations. The following is an example of the variety of characteristics that can be included in a personal description.

Race

White
Indian
Black
Asian
Chicano
other, specify

Hair Color

black
light brown
dark brown
blonde
dyed
gray
partially gray
red
white
auburn
streaked

Facial Scars

length
shape
placement
left/right cheek
chin
left/right ear
eyebrow
forehead
nose

Ears

protruding
large
small
close to head
pierced

Nose

broken, crooked
broad
straight
hooked
large
small
thin
upturned

Complexion

dark, swarthy
light, fair
medium
ruddy
sallow
tan
leathery
soft skin

Hair Type

bald
partially bald
bushy
very short
curly
kinky
straight
thin or receding
wavy
long
style, specify

Build

thin
very thin
muscular
stocky
very heavy
beer belly

Body Scars on

arm, head, neck, chest,
wrist, fingers, left or
right...

Teeth

false

caps or gaps

straight

irregular

missing

protruding

stained

decayed

chipped

Face

thin or broad

round

long

high cheek bones

hollow cheeked

chin (receding or protruding)

thin or thick lips

Eye Color

black

brown

blue

hazel

gray

green

Eye Descriptions

bulging

sunken

dark circles

cataracts

squints

blinks

stares

Facial Marks

birthmarks

freckles

pimples, moles

pockmarks

Voice

lisps

mumbles

refined speech

soft or low

stutters

accent (specify)

deep

raspy

loud

shouts

sound drops off

enunciates well

Walk

smooth

flat footed

stomps

limps

bow-legged

struts

Height

very short:
(under 5'2")

short:
(5'2"-5'6")

medium:
(5'7"-5'9")

tall:
(5'10"-6'1")

very tall:
(over 6'2")

Face Hair

thin, light

heavy, bushy

sideburns

unshaven

beard/mustache

color

shadow

Age

young,

mature,

elderly

in 20s, 30s, 40s...

Other Physical

tattoos (where, what)

body odor

Clothing

earrings

watch

other jewelry

reg/sun glasses

gloves

shoes

socks

uniform

sloppy

dirty

fashionable

coat, sweater

pants, shirt

hat or cap

color

baggy, tight

Approach

asks for advice
asks for help
claims to be_____
follows person
meets at party
goes on a date
offers job, gifts...
delivers insults
invites person in for coffee
acts like friend
touches
stands too close

Conversation

apologetic
abusive language
uses obscenities
polite
reveals hostilities
talkative
threatens
silent
makes jokes
full sentences
vulgar/profane
talks rapidly
laughs
direct language
hints around
gestures
smooth talker

Safety Planning

Planning ahead for our safety can greatly improve our chances for avoiding, deterring, escaping, and surviving assault. It can be a way to transform our fears into practical ideas that make the anxiety producing circumstances feel manageable. The following guidelines can prepare us for upcoming encounters that are likely to be difficult or dangerous and scenarios that cause fear or anxiety. Include settings that involve people you know who produce feelings of distrust or discomfort. Use real situations, ones described in this Appendix, or make up your own.

1. Describe a situation and include many details. Who will be there? Who may be nearby? Where will it be? Can it be somewhere else? When will it happen? What will happen? What is the greatest danger? What is the biggest fear? Make separate lists of what may realistically happen and what you fear may happen.

2. List many precautionary and defense options that you would want to use in the situation above according to the following categories. Use the options listed in this Appendix for ideas. Try to address all the information collected above. The more options a woman uses, the greater her chances of controlling the situation.

    a. *Prevention* — Identify self-care and personal support options. Gather accurate information about the situation and what might happen. Include details about escape routes, weapons of convenience, and people who may come to your aid if needed. Think about options that exercise your control over the circumstances before any sign of danger appears.

    b. *Avoidance* — List tactics that can be initiated when intuition warns that the assailant is considering assault. Include options that communicate confidence and assertiveness, strategies that involve others, and ways to leave.

    c. *Deterrence* — When the assailant begins to assert dominance in the situation, what options are you willing to use? Be specific. Think of the exact words you want to say, how you will sit or stand, where you will look, what you will do, who you will call, how they can help, and where you can go. Any action that communicates confidence and an unwillingness to be overpowered will be an advantage.

d. *Escape* — Among the range of escape strategies described in Chapter 6, choose the ones you consider appropriate for this situation. Pick several and describe them in detail. The main principle is to use your strengths against the assailants weaknesses, both psychological and physical.

e. *Survival* — Review the strategies that help you hold on to your sense of strength, dignity, and self-worth. List the tactics you want to use to help you endure the situation and options that will keep your mind actively making decisions.

3. Draw the line that signifies the need to move into the next level of options. Define your feelings or what the assailant must do before you initiate avoidance, deterrence, or escape options.

4. Practice and visualize yourself successfully carrying out the options listed. Watch yourself practicing in a mirror to check that your face, body, voice, and words communicate the same thing. Practice with others who will be involved in the situation, if applicable. Supportive friends and family can help roleplay the situation, give valuable feedback, and provide more ideas to choose from. The more the mind (through visualization) and the body (through physical practice) repeat what you want to do, the greater the chances are that your choices will be successful.

5. You may feel so confident after doing this planning that you decide to try other options in the real situation. Or, for whatever reason, your tactics are not working as planned. Perhaps they slip your mind. Remember that you do not have to follow the plan. No matter what happens with your plan, you will do the best you can in the situation. Whatever an assailant does to you is not your fault.

Situations for Practice and Safety Planning

Practicing strategies and roleplaying situations, real or fictitious, helps us learn new defensive responses and be more prepared emotionally and tactically to deal with similar circumstances. The following variety of situations can be used to develop safety plans and practice confident body posture, the Broken Record, other verbal responses, mean intent, yelling, fighting strategies, or other options.

Alter these scenarios to make them realistic for you or use them to make up your own. Use the Safety Planning process outlined in this Appendix and practice many different options. Repeat them until they feel comfortable. Practice alone, in front of a mirror, using a tape recorder or video camera, or with a supportive friend.

- You are enjoying a moment of peace and quiet alone at a park or in a cafe. A person you recognize from work or school but do not know well comes by and starts a conversation. You really do not want to talk to him. Consider different ways to end the conversation quickly.

- Your boss, co-worker, or teacher asks you to do a personal favor or eat lunch with him. His manner feels inappropriate to you. Use verbal responses and options that respond to different levels of threat and aggression.

- A neighbor comes over to visit and learns that you live alone. He starts to come over often and is beginning to make you uncomfortable. Practice varying responses for different kinds of behavior from this neighbor including personal questions, touches and sexual advances.

- A salesman comes to your door with a product you want to buy. You are alone. Try different ways to answer the door and purchase the product while taking safety precautions.

- At work, school, bar, or a party, you meet a man who seems very nice. You do not know him well but would like to get better acquainted. He wants to drive you home. Establish your limits with men in this kind of situation, think about precautions, decide on ways you will and will not socialize with men you do not know well, and practice what you would like to say and do.

- You are a woman who is blind or deaf. You ask a co-worker, sales clerk, teacher, or stranger for directions to the restroom. This person insists on showing you the way by grabbing your arm. You only need directions and do not want your arm held. Think of ways to present a strong body posture and strategies for communicating assertively.

- Your date insists on paying all the expenses for the evening. He begins to make sexual advances and seems hurt when you tell him to stop because you do not want him to touch you in this way. He says, "I do a lot for you. I take you out and give you a good time. All I want is to touch you a little." Practice different verbal responses and decide when your date's behavior will warrant you to escalate your defensive measures.

- On the bus, a man sits next to you and starts a friendly conversation. After awhile, he asks you where you get off the bus, where you work, what street you live on, and other kinds of personal information. Think about the personal information you feel comfortable sharing with strangers or acquaintances you do not know well. Decide what your limits are. Public knowledge of some types of information can make you more vulnerable.

- A man makes rude comments and obscene gestures at you while you wait in line for food at a burger stand. He won't leave you alone. At what point will you involve others, make a scene, tell the management, or call the police? What else can you do?

- While entering a quiet and deserted parking garage to get your car, you feel an eerie, uncomfortable sensation. Options can include ways to involve others, letting out a fierce roar while approaching your car, parking in a different area of the garage that feels more safe in the future, and approaching the garage ownership for safety improvements.

- At a family gathering, you notice that the uncle who has always made you uncomfortable continues to give you an uneasy feeling. He approaches you for quiet conversation away from the crowd. Roleplay several options, including ones that may cause "a scene".

- There have been reports of repeated assaults occurring outdoors at night in your neighborhood. Include your neighbors, if possible, in your plans and practice of options that range from prevention to survival.

- After a stressful day at work your partner, roommate, or husband frequently abuses you verbally and physically. You just called the office and discovered that major budget cuts were announced that afternoon and everyone had just left for the day. Safety and defensive plans and options can be short-term and/or long-term.

- You are being followed down a hall, outside, or in the mall. Consider where you can go, what you can do, how other people can be involved, and what you will say.

- You have separated from your abusive roommate, partner, or husband and have managed to cut communication for many months. However, the two of you must meet soon to make some final arrangements. Figure out options that can give you more control in the situation such as insisting on setting the time and location of the meeting. Make a list of what might happen and make a detailed plan of response.

- You tell someone in your family that you have been assaulted. She says, "I can't believe it. This just couldn't happen to you! Did you do anything about it?" Think about what you want to say to her about her inappropriate response, other options for getting the help you need, and ways you can care for yourself.

Self-Defense Options

This list of options is created as a starting point. It shows the wide range of options women can choose to feel safer or resist violence. Hopefully, these tactics will trigger your memory or creativity so that more strategies can be added. Make this your list. All options may not be suitable for everyone. We must choose among them based on the situation, our individual emotional needs, moral standards, and physical abilities. Women with disabilities can effectively use most of these options. Some can be adapted to be more useful. Others may hold more importance for women with limited ability. We can use this list to creatively expand the range of options we find appropriate and are able to use.

Prevention: Self-Care, Personal Support, Accurate Information, and Preparation

- Do things that help us feel confident, appreciated, and worthy.

- Actively work on emotional issues, perhaps with a counselor, that affect self-esteem and confidence.

- Schedule a minimum of thirty minutes a day to do things just for yourself.

- Eat, sleep, and get enough exercise to feel healthy.

- Work toward the ability to be financially independent.

- Find people to include in a personal support network that will help in circumstances regarding safety when you need them.

- Read, attend workshops, or call a local agency that supports women who are abused or assaulted for accurate information about assault.

- Make the effort to learn about assault, the cycles of violence, continuums of domestic abuse, and how to break these cycles.

- Talk about these issues with supportive friends, family members, or others.

- Get involved in exercise, dance, or sports.

- Take a self-defense class.

- Identify people we know who might be abusers, assailants, or harassers and make safety plans for situations involving them.

- Practice tactics and strategies that we want to use in future situations.

- Be assertive at work, with friends, and in other relationships that are not threatening or dangerous.

- Keep a journal of intuitive messages. Verify them for accuracy and try to consciously use intuition in more areas of life.

- Learn to use and practice fighting skills with the strong parts of our bodies.

- Use the steps outlined in Chapter 6 for effective yelling when calling kids or pets to return home.

- Give our kids accurate information about assault and discuss safety strategies by playing "What If...?"

- Learn about and model non-violent methods of dealing with anger, disagreements, problems, and frustration.

- Know our neighbors.

- Consider how certain kinds of clothes can hinder or help in situations when we might decide to run or fight.

- Be honest in all communications, setting a tone that tells others that when we say "No", we mean "No".

Avoidance: Taking Action as Soon as There is an Awareness of Possible Assault Through Our Intuition or the Behavior of Others

- Talk to trusted neighbors, family and friends to create a safety plan that outlines what they will do when a certain person arrives, we call and give a coded message, they hear us whistle three times...

- Think about the security in our homes. Be sure to consider how we can quickly get out as well as keeping intruders from entering. In addition to locks, security can also include lights, a dog, and alarms. Even landscaping can be important if it can hide intruders or if prickly bushes can impede them.

- Get a full tank of gas.

- Stay alert with all possible physical and intuitive senses to improve awareness.

- Notice escape routes, people who may be able to help, weapons of opportunity.

- Change the location of a meeting to a more public place.

- Invite others to the situation.

- Be careful to not divulge personal information like last name, address, phone number, and workplace to people who make us uncomfortable or in situations we are not sure about.

- Get the boss, school administration, or city to put bright lights in the parking lot.

- Provide our own transportation and carry enough money for our own expenses on dates we are not sure about.

- Find out if people who make us feel uncomfortable will be at a party or function we plan to attend.

- Carry a loud whistle.

- Ask people for directions without giving our exact destinations.

- Decline assistance from people who give us feelings of discomfort or uncertainty.
- Find alternatives to isolated corridors, stairways, and streets.
- Tell visitors and repair people to inform us in advance of their arrival.
- Talk to salespeople or strangers through a closed, locked door.
- Yell, "I'll get it, dear," before answering the door when home alone.
- Before using a laundry room, going somewhere that feels dangerous, or doing something where we may be vulnerable, inform a neighbor, person we live with, someone at our destination, or a friend so they can look for us if a certain amount of time elapses before we arrive or call.
- If hearing is a problem, use a peephole to answer the door, and pass a message through the space under the door if the person is not well known.
- Park the car where there are people, lights, and escape routes.
- If followed, drive to a busy, crowded place.
- Cross the street or walk in the street.
- Go into a crowded store.

Deterrence: De-Escalating the Situation Once the Assailant Begins to Assert Dominance

- Stand or sit tall and straight, look him in the eye, and express our needs in short, clear phrases.
- End the conversation and leave.
- Get a restraining or protection order.
- Walk in the middle of the street.
- Be willing to risk embarrassment, possibly being wrong, or over-reacting.

- If we are being followed, step aside and let the person go by, go into a public place, or confront him.
- Stick to our decisions, even in small or unimportant issues. Abusers often want compliance on many issues that may seem trivial when considered individually but the broad picture shows them gaining total control.
- Let our loud, assertive statements be overheard.
- Stand up immediately if the situation began in a sitting or prone position.
- Tell the assailant we are sick, at high risk of a heart attack, or have asthma which gets serious when we are under stress.
- Call a co-worker, acquaintance, friend, or stranger to join the encounter.
- Go up to a stranger and make conversation as if the stranger was a long lost friend.
- Initiate the safety plan made with a neighbor by using a code everyone agreed will mean that the neighbor will come over.
- Run.
- Ignore the situation while maintaining confident body posture.
- Stall by negotiating.
- Say things that make no sense what-so-ever.
- Make fun of the assailant.
- Initiate a prearranged safety plan involving your children that directs them to make noise, call the police, or run to a neighbor for help.
- If we are in a car and the assailant is outside, start the engine and drive away.
- If we are in the car with the assailant, reach for the horn and keep honking it. If we are driving, screech to a halt and order him to get out.
- If followed, drive to a busy, crowded place.

Escape: Doing Whatever is Necessary in Order to Leave Quickly

- Yell.
- Repeat assertive statements with mean intent, big gestures, and a very loud voice.
- Concentrate continually on escape.
- Throw up, spit, or engage in other gross behavior.
- Laugh hysterically.
- Drive the car to the police or fire department's front door.
- If we are driving with the assailant also in the car, honk the horn, run into garbage cans and over curbs, or drive on the side walk.
- Spray hair spray, deodorant, household cleaner, or spray device like mace into the assailant's eyes.
- Call the police.
- Get a divorce.
- Point to a stranger and yell, "You with the hat [or other distinguishing characteristic], call the police."
- Tell the assailant that a repair person is expected to arrive momentarily, even if no one is coming.
- Blow a loud, piercing, whistle.
- Use the strong parts of our bodies to strike the assailant's targets: eyes, nose, throat, groin, or knees.
- Use whatever is handy to strike the assailant's targets.
- Follow-up a strike with another strike to the same target or another target.
- Yell while striking and showing mean intent.
- Follow-up a strike with a yell or non-physical tactic.
- If we are held, wait to strike when an arm or leg becomes free.
- Run.

- Analyze how we are being held to locate available targets on the assailant and strong parts of our bodies to strike them with.
- Bite, scratch, pull hair, or whatever else will cause pain in a sensitive area.
- Use a gun or knife.
- Put an object in the path of a strike to avoid being hit.
- Throw open drawers and doors and tip over chairs and garbage to make it difficult for the assailant to chase quickly.

Survival: Enduring While Maintaining Dignity and Self-Worth

- Think of "giving in" as "waiting" instead.
- Take advantage of opportunities to make new choices when possible.
- Focus on amassing details of the situation for later prosecution of the assailant.
- Repeat aloud or to ourselves, "This is not my fault. I am doing the best I can. I am a good person. I will survive."
- Visualize the people we love, feel them caring for us, and make plans to get support from them as soon as the ordeal is over.
- Think about the important things we do and the things we like to do. Focus on getting back to doing those things right away.
- Draw on an image that gives energy, courage, and the determination to persist.
- Hold onto that place inside each one of us which no one can touch, invade, degrade, or destroy. Remember that because of this place, no assailant can completely overpower us.
- Contact support people or organizations.
- Do not let others convince us that the assault was our fault or we could have resisted it better.

- Report the assailant to authorities if we want to and feel it will be empowering.

- If one source of help does not feel supportive, go to someone else until the support needed is found.

Men's Role in Ending Assault Against Women

Even an educated, socially enlightened, and cultured man, says Timothy Beneke, in his book Men On Rape, can live his life without thinking about "something fundamental in his experience: women live in social environments far more menacing than men. He can even become a successful psychiatrist and never perceive that the threat of rape constitutes a major mental health issue for all women in American culture."

Beneke calls on men to rethink their relationships with women. Men need to respect women as the human beings they are, reject the acceptance of restrictions placed on women's lives due to the threat of violence as normal, stop blaming women for the assaults they experience, and put their anger at women aside.

For violence against women to end, Beneke states that men must perceive this violence as a man's problem, "one that results directly from the way men regard women in American culture." This cannot begin until men stop blaming women for their assaults. Men must not only understand the crimes involved, says Beneke, but also comprehend how the threat of assault affects women in almost every aspect of their lives. He encourages men to listen to women talk about their experiences and feelings regarding the violence they face.

"For men who care about women or (finally) themselves, violence against women benefits no one. It mystifies and poisons relations between men and women and vitiates the potential for trust, love, and surrender," concludes Beneke. He is convinced that men will take action to end this violence once they listen to women and wake up to the reality of the violence women face.

FIST has met men who want to help end violence against women but are unsure of how to participate. Many rape crisis centers, women's shelters, assault prevention programs, and support groups for assault survivors are for women only, for good reasons. One is to take back the sense of power and control that women lose when living with and facing violence at the hands of men. However, men need to be actively involved in ending violence against women because this violence will not stop until they stop abusing, assaulting, and harassing women. The following are some ways men can work toward a violence-free future.

- Speak out publicly against assault. Find a group working on this issue with a speaker's bureau and join.

- Talk with other men about changing sexist behavior. Much of this behavior is also sexual harassment. It contributes to "rape culture", a culture where rape and abuse are condoned.

- Think about one's own behavior with women, other men, on dates, and with children. Include language, sexual behavior, expectations, power issues, anger management, and conflict resolution. Behavior that demeans, endangers, or does not support women's self-determination should not continue.

- Think about, discuss with other men, and avoid being involved in actions that might be interpreted or perceived as threatening by women.

- Listen objectively to the criticisms women make of male behavior.

- Avoid any form of sexual coercion in one's own sexuality. This includes frank conversations with one's sexual partner to determine mutually consenting behaviors.

- By respecting a woman's "No" to mean "No", one sets the stage for honesty in all conversations.

- Join or start a support group for men to work on changing their attitudes toward women and assault and replacing behaviors that demean, endanger, or do not support self-determination for women.

- Join or start a support group for male survivors of sexual assault.

- Be a positive role model for children.

- Learn about the myths that shroud the realities of assault against women. Many myths are surprisingly difficult to discard. Work to grasp the realities in order to speak knowledgeably about the issue and support people who have survived assault.

- Support women in their efforts to end the violence they face by offering personal support, backing the decisions they make, and following through with their requests.

- Join or start a group for men to support women's organizations working on these issues.

Resources

Locating Services

To find services for women related to sexual and domestic violence, look in the telephone book for a section listing community services. It will usually include local women's shelters, domestic violence or rape crisis centers, and hot lines. In the yellow pages, these services may also be listed under crisis intervention services or social service organizations.

If there are no listings for your locality, other organizations may be able to help. Community mental health centers, student services at local colleges, women's centers and health clinics, and other social service agencies may have lists of organizations and individuals for referral. A domestic violence or sexual assault center in a neighboring location is also a good resource.

Workers against sexual assault and domestic violence have organized across the nation and established national offices. These coalitions can make referrals across the country.

National Coalition Against Domestic Violence
P.O. Box 34103, Washington, D.C. 20043-4103
202/638-7388

National Domestic Violence Hotline: 1-800-333-SAFE
This number can be called for initial counseling and a supportive ear as well as referrals.

National Coalition Against Sexual Assault
P.O. Box 21378, Washington, D.C. 20009
202/483-7165

Self-Defense Classes

Taking a self-defense class should be an empowering, enlightening, and fun experience. Too often, classes do not meet women's expectations. The following are some ideas for finding a self-defense class to meet your needs.

As discussed in this book, self-defense and martial art are often considered interchangeable. Part of the confusion is because most martial arts have a "self-defense" component which is the practical application of the martial art's techniques. This usually focuses on physical fighting skills and generally requires more instruction, practice, and skill than self-defense classes not associated with a martial art. Most martial arts focus on fitness, sport, and philosophy rather than emphasizing assault prevention and resistance. Their study can be very rewarding but being proficient takes a commitment of time and practice.

General self-defense classes focus on practical aspects of resisting assault. Content, length, and teaching styles vary widely and offer women many choices. A large number of programs are based on physical techniques and assume that assailants will be strangers. A focus on strategies for completely incapacitating assailants is not uncommon. Some programs mainly present information on home security or firearms. Assertiveness classes may be designed for assault prevention or focus on workplace and relationship issues. Self-defense programs created by women are more likely to cover practical strategies for situations women commonly face and incorporate emotional, psychological, and social issues in addition to physical techniques.

Many general self-defense classes are taught by police officers and martial artists who branch outside their art to offer its practical aspects to the general community. Watch out for self-defense teachers who give lots of advice, tell women what and what not to do, focus primarily on stranger assault, and may not completely believe that all women have the capacity to resist assault.

To find a program that meets your needs, ask questions, observe classes, find out about the instructor's training, and read the literature from different programs. Talk to the instructor and students to get a sense of the instructor's knowledge about violence against women and the attitude displayed about women learning self-defense. Listen to your intuition. Information on self-defense programs created by women is usually available at agencies supporting survivors of rape and domestic violence, women's shelter programs, women's bookstores, and women's centers in colleges or in the community. Other programs are usually listed in phone books, through city or college recreation bulletins, or advertised in local newspapers.

Books

Information About Assault

Against Our Will: Men, Women And Rape, Susan Brownmiller, Bantam Books, New York, 1976.

This is the book that raised people's consciousness about rape.

Chain Chain Change: For Black Women Dealing With Physical And Emotional Abuse, Evelyn White, Seal Press, Seattle, WA, 1985.

Information on domestic violence, abuse and its effect on children, and advice on dealing with authorities are provided in this short book written for black women.

Conspiracy Of Silence: The Trauma Of Incest, Sandra Butler, New Glide, San Francisco, 1978.

This book is considered the authority on incest.

Handbook Of Family Violence, Vincent B. Van Hasselt, et al., Plenum, Press, New York, 1988.

Information on the high incidence of family violence in the United States is presented in this collection of professional articles which include indexes and bibliographies.

I Never Called It Rape: The Ms. Report On Recognizing, Fighting, And Surviving Date and Acquaintance Rape, Robin Warshaw, Harper & Row, New York, 1988.

A study of 6,159 male and female college students forms the basis for this readable, contemporary account of date and acquaintance rape. It also contains a resource list of books, videotapes, films, program guides, conferences, and organizations.

Mad At Miles: A Blackwoman's Guide To Truth, Pearl Cleage, The
Cleage Group (1-800-325-6524), Southfield, MA, 1990.
    This short discussion about violence against women with some
    tips on what to do about it combines issues of sexism, racism,
    feminism, and oppression.

Men On Rape, Timothy Beneke, St. Martin's Press, New York, 1982.
    Interviews with men from many backgrounds about sexual
    violence provides startling insight into why men rape. Beneke
    clearly states why and how men should stand up against sexual
    assault.

Sexual Exploitation: Rape, Child Sexual Abuse, and Workplace
    Harassment, Diana E. H. Russell, Sage Publications, Beverly Hills,
    CA, 1984.
    Well documented information on sexual violence and its causes is
    drawn from many professional papers and books.

Sexual Violence: The Unmentionable Sin, Marie M. Fortune, Pilgrim
Press, New York, 1983.
    Marie Fortune is a reverend who is a leader in the movement to
    end violence against women.

Women And Male Violence: The Visions And Struggles Of The
    Battered Women's Movement, Susan Schechter, South End Press,
    Boston, MA, 1982.
    Based on interviews with women involved in the battered
    women's movement, Schechter describes the movement's history
    in the United States, its current progress and problems.

Self-Defense

Attitude: Commonsense Defense For Women, Lisa Sliwa, Crown
    Publishers, Inc., New York, 1986.
    Lisa, a leader of the Guardian Angels based in New York City, has
    very strong opinions about what women should do. However, her
    experience in big city streets with street punks and gangs gives
    practical insight into defense strategies against strangers and
    typical big city thugs.

Choices: Sexual Assault Prevention Workbook For Persons Who Are
    Deaf And Hard Of Hearing, Ellen Shaman, Seattle Rape Relief
    (1825 S. Jackson, Suite 102, Seattle, WA, 206/325-5531), 1985.
    This workbook is practical and has good information about sexual
    assault and its prevention.

Choices: Sexual Assault Prevention Workbook For Persons With Physical Disabilities, Ellen Shaman, Seattle Rape Relief (1825 S. Jackson, Suite 102, Seattle, WA, 206/325-5531), 1985.

This workbook is practical and has good information about sexual assault and its prevention.

Choices: Sexual Assault Prevention Workbook For Persons With Visual Impairments, Ellen Shaman, Seattle Rape Relief (1825 S. Jackson, Suite 102, Seattle, WA, 206/325-5531), 1985.

This workbook is practical and has good information about sexual assault and its prevention.

Getting Free: A Handbook For Women In Abusive Relationships, Ginny NiCarthy, The Seal Press, Seattle, WA, 1986.

Sections on making the decision to leave or stay in a relationship, getting professional help, helping yourself survive, and life after leaving the relationship thoroughly cover the many issues women face when living with abuse and deciding what to do. A new section in this second edition includes information about teen, lesbian, and emotional abuse.

Her Wits About Her: Self-Defense Success Stories By Women, Denise Caignon and Gail Groves, Harper and Row, New York, 1987.

This book is a collection of success stories told by women in many different situations. It contains excellent information on assault in general and self-defense. A list of self-defense programs and an excellent bibliography concludes it.

In Defense Of Ourselves: A Rape Prevention Handbook For Women, Linda Tschirhart Sanford and Ann Fetter, Doubleday & Company, Garden City, NY, 1979.

This is one of the first books on the subject written from a woman's perspective. Self-defense options focus on physical fighting skills but information on media, female socialization, self-esteem, and applications for teen, elderly, rural, lesbian, and developmentally disabled women, women of color, and survivors make this book useful and insightful. It is out of print but available in libraries.

Self-Assertion For Women, Pamela E. Butler, Harper & Row, New York, 1981.

Easy to read and informative, this book encourages women to accept our own feelings as valid and legitimate.

Sixth Sense: The Whole-brain Book Of Intuition, Hunches, Gut
    Feelings, And Their Place In Your Everyday Life, Laurie Nadel,
    Prentice Hall Press, New York, 1990.
    This up-to-date book helps people recognize, trust, and use
    intuition.

Stopping Rape: Successful Survival Strategies, Pauline B. Bart and
    Patricia H. O'Brien, Pergamon Press, Elmsford, NY, 1985.
    Material for this book was drawn from Bart's research on women
    who avoided rape. It presents a number of successful strategies.

Women's Self-Defense: A Complete Guide To Assault Prevention,
    Rosanna Hill, Joan Iten Sutherland, and Patricia Giggans, Los
    Angeles Commission on Assaults Against Women (543 N. Fairfax
    Ave., Los Angeles, CA, 90036), 1987.
    This self-defense guide covers many aspects of resisting assault
    including lots of physical techniques. It has short sections on
    handling emotions, information for assault survivors, and self-
    defense for elderly, deaf, blind, and disabled women.

For Kids and Parents

Childproof For Sexual Abuse, Parent Education Center of Yakima
    (4823 Snow Mountain Rd, Yakima, WA, 98908).
    This booklet has sections on how and why to talk to children,
    normal sexual development, and activities for parents to use with
    their children. It was designed for use in discussions among small
    groups of parents.

Feeling Safe Feeling Strong: How To Avoid Sexual Abuse And What
    To Do If It Happens To You, Susan Terkel & Janice Rench, Lerner
    Publications Company, Minneapolis, MN, 1984.
    Fictional vignettes written for older children illustrate different
    kinds of sexual abuse commonly experienced by children. Al-
    though the stories portray touching problems caused by family
    and acquaintances, its short chapter on rape misleadingly focuses
    on strangers.

It Happens To Boys, Too, Jane A.W. Satullo, Roberta Russell, and Pat
    A. Bradway, Rape Crisis Center of the Berkshires Press (18 Charles
    St., Pittsfield, MA, 01201), 1987.
    Sexual assault information for elementary school age boys is the
    focus of this book.

It's MY Body: A Book To Teach Young Children How To Resist
Uncomfortable Touch, Lory Freeman, Parenting Press Inc. (7744
31st Ave. NE, Seattle, 98115), 1982.
This book teaches young children to make choices about touches
they receive.

My Very Own Book About Me, Jo Stowell and Mary Dietzel, Rape
Crisis Network, Lutheran Social Services of WA (N. 1226 Howard,
Spokane, WA, 99201), 1981.
This is a workbook for elementary school age kids with illustrations which kids can decorate and color. It gives parents and
children a comfortable way to talk about sexual abuse and comes
with a parent and teacher guide.

No Is Not Enough: Helping Teenagers Avoid Sexual Assault, Caren
Adams, Jennifer Fay, and Jan Loreen-Martin, Impact Publishers,
San Luis Obisbo, CA, 1984.
This practical and comprehensive book for parents of teenagers
includes chapters on talking with teens, self-esteem, sex role
expectations, avoiding abuse in relationships, family stress, and
how to respond if your teen is assaulted.

No More Secrets: Protecting Your Child From Sexual Assault, Caren
Adams and Jennifer Fay, Impact Publishers, San Luis Obispo, CA,
1981.
Many questions about protecting children from sexual assault are
discussed such as where to begin, what to say, and when to say it.
Chapters also include clues for identifying a child who has been
assaulted and what to do if your child is assaulted.

Planned Parenthood distributes pamphlets for parents about assaults
against children.

Safe, Strong & Streetwise, Helen Benedict, Little, Brown and Company, 1987.
Issues and common scenarios such as dates, parties, and dealing
with parents make this book about sexual assault prevention
practical for teenagers. There are many good ideas and safety tips
but readers must remember they are options, not rules.

So What's It To Me?, Gail Stringer, King County Sexual Assault
Resource Center (P.O. Box 300, Renton, WA, 98057, 206/226-5062),
1987.
This book for teen boys explores issues of sexuality and has a
section for male victims.

The Silent Children: A Parent's Guide To The Prevention Of Child Sexual Abuse, Linda Tschirhart Sanford, Anchor Press, Doubleday, Garden City, NY, 1980.

Background information on child sexual assault is presented as well as ideas for raising children to resist assault by building self-esteem, developing confidence, and saying no. Chapters written by parents of kids of color and disabled kids give some attention to their special needs.

Top Secret: Sexual Assault Information For Teenagers Only, Jennifer J. Fay and Billie Jo Flerchinger, King County Rape Relief (P.O. Box 300, Renton, WA, 98057, 206/226-5062), 1982.

Written and designed just for teens, this short book tells their stories and answers their questions about many aspects regarding sexual assault.

Recovering from Assault

Coping With Date Rape & Acquaintance Rape, Andrea Parrot, The Rosen Publishing Group, New York, 1988.

This short book gives survivors of date and acquaintance rape information about their assault, feelings common for survivors, and where to go for help.

Courage To Heal: A Guide For Women Survivors Of Child Sexual Abuse, Ellen Bass and Laura Davis, Harper & Row, New York, 1988.

Complete with writing exercises and a separate workbook (The Courage To Heal Workbook For Women And Men Survivors Of Child Sexual Abuse, Laura Davis, Harper & Row, 1990), this readable and supportive manual is full of information and stories from survivors that guide readers through the healing process. The workbook includes exercises for building a support system and nurturing ourselves as well as activities for many other aspects of healing.

Quest For Respect: A Healing Guide For Survivors Of Rape, Linda Braswell, Pathfinder Publishing, Ventura, CA, 1989.

Helping rape survivors restore their personal power and heal their spirits is the purpose of this little book.

Recovering From Rape, Linda Ledray, Henry Holt And Company, New York, 1986.

Practical information is provided on many issues related to recovering from assault. It is written for survivors and their families, lovers, and friends.

Recovery: How To Survive Sexual Assault For Women, Men, Teenagers, Their Friends And Families, Helen Benedict, Doubleday & Company, Garden City, NY, 1985.

Thorough and supportive coverage of issues for survivors include helping yourself, how others can help, and prosecuting. There are listings of resources by state and special sections covering marital rape and rape experienced by older women, teens, men, lesbians, and gay men.

Service Directories

Webster, Linda, ed., Sexual Assault And Child Sexual Abuse: A National Directory Of Victim/Survivor Services And Prevention Programs, Phoenix, AZ, Oryx Press, 1989.

This directory is useful for finding services dealing with sexual assault and abuse. Organized by state, it includes approximately 2,700 local agencies, 268 state agencies and organizations, and 100 national organizations.

E

F

P

R

S

FIST welcomes your comments. To correspond with FIST, write:

FIST

P.O. Box 1883

Olympia, WA 98507 USA

R&M Press can be reached by writing:

R&M Press

625 Commerce Street Suite 100

Tacoma, WA 98402-4601 USA